A CARDINAL NEWMAN PRAYERBOOK

A CARDINAL NEWMAN PRAYERBOOK

Kindly Light

Compiled from His Writings by

DANIEL M. O'CONNELL, S.J.

DIMENSION BOOKS
Denville, New Jersey 07834

Published by Dimension Books, Inc. P.O. Box 811, Denville, New Jersey. Thanks are due to America Press, the original Publisher, and to the Editor, Father Daniel M. O'Connell, S.J. who died on July 29, 1959.

ISBN 0-87193-220-2

Nihil Obstat   Arthur J. Scanlan

Imprimatur   + Francis J. Spellman Archbishop of New York

CONTENTS

SUGGESTED DAILY DEVOTION

Morning and Evening Reflections

SUNDAY

The Holy Trinity. Pages 4-11; 83-95; 136-141; 197-200; 297-300

MONDAY

The Hidden Life. 3; 16-21; 44-46; 103-114; 264-266

TUESDAY

The Public Life. 51-59; 96-100; 216-222; 241-244

WEDNESDAY

The Risen Life. 60-71; 82; 121-134; 168-176; 278-280

THURSDAY

Special Prayers. 8-10; 22; 41-50; 86-88; 162-167; 273-277; 329

FRIDAY

Our Lord's Sufferings. 34-35; 47-48; 115-120; 134-135; 157-161; 246-252; 281-284; 309

SATURDAY

Angels, Saints; Their Queen. 78-81; 142; 146-156; 194; 267-269; 301-307; 317; 322

SELECTIONS BY SEASONS
OF THE YEAR

I

THE WAY

Let me set my thoughts on things above, and in His own good time God will set my affections on things above.

BY FAITH

EVER since the Eternal Son of God was born in a stable, and had not a place to lay His head, and died an outcast and as a malefactor, heaven has been won by poverty, by disgrace, and by suffering. Not by these things in themselves, but by faith working in and through them. "Jesus, meek and humble of Heart, make our hearts like unto Thine."

SONS OF GOD

THIS be our duty in the dark night, while we wait for the day; while we wait for Him who is our Day, while we wait for His coming, who is gone, who will return, and before whom all the tribes of the earth will mourn, but the sons of God will rejoice. "It hath not yet appeared what we shall be. We know that, when He shall appear, we shall be like to Him: because we shall see Him as He is. And every one that hath this hope in Him sanctifieth himself, as He also is holy."

OUR BLESSEDNESS

IT IS our blessedness to be made like the all-holy, all gracious, long-suffering, and merciful God; who made and who redeemed us; in whose presence is perfect rest, and perfect peace; whom the Seraphim are harmoniously praising, and the Cherubim tranquilly contemplating and Angels silently serving, and the Church thankfully worshipping. All is order, repose, love, and holiness in heaven. There is no anxiety, no ambition, no resentment, no discontent, no bitterness, no remorse, no tumult. "Thou wilt keep peace: because we have hoped in Thee . . . in the Lord God, mighty forever."

WONDERFUL MYSTERY

THUS was it, we are told, from everlasting;—before the heavens and the earth were made, before man fell or Angels rebelled, before the sons of God were formed in the morning of creation, yea, before there were Seraphim to veil their faces before Him and cry "Holy." He existed without ministers, without attendants,

[4]

without court and kingdom, without manifested glory, without anything but Himself; He His own Temple, His own infinite rest, His own supreme bliss, from eternity. O wonderful mystery!

DWELT WITHOUT

O THE DEPTH of His majesty! O deep things which the Spirit only knoweth! Wonderful and strange to creatures who grovel on this earth, as we, that He, the All-powerful, the All-wise, the All-good, the All-glorious, should for an eternity, for years without end, or rather, apart from time, which is but one of His creatures, that He should have dwelt without those through whom He might be powerful, in whom He might be wise, towards whom He might be good, by whom be glorified.

Glory be to the Father and the Son and the Holy Ghost; as it was in the beginning, is now and ever shall be, world without end. Amen.

NOT SOLITARY

O, WONDERFUL, that all His deep and infinite attributes should have been without manifestation! O wonderful thought! and withal, O thought comfortable to us worms of the earth, as often as we feel in ourselves and see in others gifts which have no exercise, and powers which are quiescent! He, the All-powerful God, rested from eternity, and did not work; and yet, why not rest, wonderful though it be, seeing He was so blessed in Himself?

Why should He seek external objects to know, to love, and to commune with, who was all-sufficient in Himself? How could he need fellows, as though He were a man, when He was not solitary, but had ever with Him His Only-begotten Word in whom He delighted, whom He loved ineffably, and the Eternal Spirit, the very bond of love and peace, dwelling in and dwelt in by Father and Son?

How could He need fellows, who has no origin, who is all-sufficient for Himself; who created and upholds the universe? Who is an Individual, Self-dependent, All-perfect, Unchangeable?

[6]

SURROUND HIMSELF

RATHER how was it that He ever began to create, who had a Son without beginning and without imperfection, whom He could love with a perfect love? What exceeding exuberance of goodness was it that He should deign at length to surround Himself with creation, who had need of nothing, and to change His everlasting silence for the course of Providence and the conflict of good and evil!

PARTAKER

WHY should He make man in the Image of God, whose Image already was the Son, All-perfect, All-exact, without variableness, without defect, by a natural propriety and unity of substance? And when man fell, why did He not abandon or annihilate the whole race, and create others?

Why did He go so far as to begin a fresh and more wonderful dispensation towards us, and, as He had wrought marvellously in Providence, work marvellously also in grace, even sending His

Eternal Son to take on Him our fallen nature, and to purify and renew it by His union with it? Infinite as was His own blessedness, and the Son's perfection, and man's unprofitableness, yet, in His loving-kindness, He determined that unprofitable man should be a partaker of the Son's perfection and His own blessedness! "Glory be to the Father, and to the Son and to the Holy Ghost, Amen."

PRAY WITHOUT CEASING
(A Reflection)

THERE are two modes of praying mentioned in scripture; the one is prayer at set times and places, and in set forms; the other is what the text speaks of, continual or habitual prayer. The former of these is what is commonly called prayer, whether it be public or private. The other kind of praying may also be called holding communion with God, or living in God's sight, and this may be done all through the day, wherever we are, and is commanded us as the duty, or rather the characteristic, of those who are really servants and friends of Jesus Christ.

[8]

A man cannot really be religious one hour, and not religious the next. We might as well say he could be in a state of good health one hour, and in bad health the next. A man who is religious, is religious morning, noon, and night; his religion is a certain character, a mould in which his thoughts, words, and actions are cast, all forming parts of one and the same whole. He sees God in all things; every course of action he directs towards those spiritual objects which God has revealed to him; every occurrence of the day, every event, every person met with, all news which he hears, he measures by the standard of God's will.

And a person who does this may be said almost literally to pray without ceasing; for, knowing himself to be in God's presence he is continually led to address Him reverently, whom he sets always before him, in the inward language of prayer and praise, of humble confession and joyful trust.

All this, I say, any thoughtful man acknowledges from mere natural reason. To be religious is, in other words, to have the habit of prayer, or to pray always. This

[9]

is what Scripture means by doing all things to God's glory; that is, so placing God's presence and will before us, and so consistently acting with a reference to Him, that all we do becomes one body and course of obedience to grace, witnessing without ceasing to Him who made us, and whose servants we are; and in its separate parts promoting more or less directly His glory, according as each particular thing we happen to be doing admits more or less of a religious character.

God's grace dwells in us, extending its influence to every motion of the soul, and just as healthy men and strong men show their health and strength in all they do (not indeed equally in all things, but in some things more than in others, because all actions do not require or betoken the presence of that health and strength, and yet even in their step, and their voice, and their gestures, and their countenance, showing in due measure their vigour of body), so they who have the true health and strength of the soul, a clear, sober, and deep faith in Him in whom they have their being, will in all they do, nay (as St. Paul says), even whether they "eat or drink" be living in God's sight, or, in the words of the same Apostle in the text, live in ceaseless prayer.

In proportion as I grow in grace and in the knowledge of my Saviour, so shall I approximate to Him in holiness, who is my great example, and who alone of all the sons of Adam lived in the perfection of unceasing prayer. "Jesus, meek and humble of heart."

EVER-BLESSED TRINITY

THOU art the First Cause of all thought, the Father of spirits, the One Eternal Mind, the King of kings, and Lord of lords, who only hath immortality, dwelling in light unapproachable, whom no man hath seen nor can see, the incomprehensible infinite God. Amen.

Let me gain this great benefit from the mystery of the Ever-blessed Trinity. It is calculated to humble the wise in this world with the thought of what is above them, and to encourage and elevate the lowly with the thought of Almighty God, and the glories and marvels which shall one day be revealed to them.

In the Beatific Vision of God, should I through His grace be found worthy of it, I shall comprehend clearly what I now dutifully repeat and desire to know, how the Father Almighty is truly and by Himself God, the Eternal Son truly and by Himself God, and the Holy Ghost truly and by Himself God, and yet not three Gods but one God. Glory be to the Father, etc.

GODLINESS

THOU wast born, we are born. Thou art the Son of God by nature, we are the sons of God by grace; and it is Thou who hast made us such. Thou hast taken our nature, and in and through it Thou sanctifiest us. Thou art our brother by virtue of Thy incarnation, and, as St. Paul says, "Thou art not ashamed to call us brethren." (Heb. 2, 11.)

This is the wonderful economy of grace, or mystery of godliness, which should be before my mind at all times, but especially at that season, when Thou, the Most Holy, didst take upon Thyself our flesh of the pure Virgin.

Thou wast conceived of the Holy Ghost, born of the Virgin Mary. Thou dost inhabit light inaccessible. Thou art light, and in Thee there is no darkness. Thy garment, as described in the Prophet's Vision, was white as snow and the hair of Thy head "like clean wool"; Thy "throne like flames of fire: the wheels of it like a burning flame."

Thou dost belong to the poor in spirit; Thou dost belong to the persecuted; Thou art possessed by the meek; Thou dost sustain the patient. May I conquer by Thy suffering; may I advance by Thy retiring; may I be made wise through Thy foolishness. Amen.

Jesus, meek and humble of heart, make my heart like to Thine. Amen.

CONSECRATED TO HIM

HE WAS in the world from the beginning, and man worshipped other gods; He came into the world in the flesh, and the world knew Him not; He came unto His own, and His own received Him not. But He came in order to make them receive Him, know Him, worship Him.

He came to absorb this world into Himself; that, as He was light, so it might be light also. When He came, He had not a place to lay His head; but He came to make Himself a place, to make Himself a home, to make Himself houses, to fashion for Himself a glorious dwelling out of this world, which the powers of evil had taken captive.

He came in the dark, in the dark night was He born, in a cave underground; in a cave where cattle were stabled, there was He housed; in a rude manger was He laid. There first He laid His head; but He meant not, blessed be His Name! He meant not there to remain forever. He did not resign Himself to that obscurity; He came into that cave to leave it.

The King of the Jews was born to claim the kingdom;—yea, rather, the Hope of all nations and the King of the whole earth, the King of kings and Lord of lords; and He gave not sleep to His eyes or slumber to His eyelids, till He had changed His manger for a royal throne, and His grot for high palaces. Lift up your eyes, my brethren, and look around, for it is fulfilled at this day; yea, long ago, for many ages, and in many countries. Wisdom hath builded her house, she hath hewn out her seven pillars.

Where is the grot? where the grass and straw? where the unseemly furniture of that despised place? Is it possible that the Eternal Son should have been born in a hole of the earth? Was the great miracle wrought, whereby a pure and spotless Virgin brought forth God? Strange condescension undergone to secure a strange triumph! He purposed to change the earth, and He began in the lowest pit, in a place of darkness, and in the deep. All was to be by Him renewed, and He availed Himself of nothing that was, that out of nothing He might make all things. He was not born in the Temple of Jerusalem; He abhorred the palace of David; He laid Himself on the damp earth in the cold night, a light shining in a dark place, till by the virtue that went out of Him, He should create a Temple worthy of His Name.

And lo, in omen of the future, even in His cradle, the rich and wise of the earth seek Him with gold, and frankincense, and myrrh, as an offering. And He puts aside the swaddling clothes, and takes instead a coat without seam, woven from the top throughout. And He changes water into wine; and Levi feasts Him; and Zacchaeus receives Him; and Mary anoints His head.

Pass a few generations, and the whole face of things is changed; the earth is covered with His Temples; as it has been for ages. Go where you will, you find the eternal mountains hewn and fashioned into shrines where He may dwell, who was an outcast in the days of His flesh. Rivers and mines pay tribute of their richest jewels: forests are searched for their choicest woods; the skill of man is put to task to use what nature furnishes. Go through the countries where His name is known, and you will find all that is rarest and most wonderful in nature or art has been consecrated to Him. "Glory be to the Father, to the Son and to the Holy Ghost. As it was in the beginning, is now and ever shall be, world without end." Amen.

AND HE has made Him a Temple, not
only out of inanimate things, but of men
also as parts of it. Not gold and silver,
jewels and fine linen, and skill of man
to use them, make the House of God, but
worshippers, the souls and bodies of men,
whom He has redeemed. Not souls alone,
He takes possession of the whole man,
body as well as soul; for St. Paul says,
"I beseech you, therefore, brethren, by the
mercy of God, that you present your bodies
a living sacrifice, holy, pleasing unto God,
your reasonable service."

And He claims us as His own, not one
by one, but altogether, as one great company; for St. Peter says, that we "as living
stones, are built up a spiritual house, a
holy priesthood, to offer up spiritual sacri-
fices, acceptable to God by Jesus Christ."
All of us, and every one, and every part
of every one, must go to make up His mys-
tical body; for the Psalmist says, "My
heart is ready: O God, I will sing and
will give praise. I will praise Thee, O
Lord, among the people and I will sing
unto Thee among the nations." Our

tongues must preach Him, and our voices sing of Him, and our knees adore Him, and our hands supplicate Him, and our heads bow before Him, and our countenances beam of Him, and our gait herald Him. Amen.

THY GLORY

"THE TIME is short." It is very plain that matters which agitate me most extremely now, will then interest me not at all; that objects about which I have intense hope and fear now, will then be to me nothing more than things which happen at the other end of the earth.

They will have no life in them; they will be as faded flowers of a banquet, which do but mock me. Or when I lie on the bed of death, what will it avail me to have been rich or great or fortunate or honored or influential? All things will then be vanity.

Let me be negligent of this world, be unexcited, be singleminded, "looking for the blessed hope and coming of the glory of the great God and our Saviour, Jesus Christ." Amen.

[18]

THE WORLD UNSEEN

THEY ALONE are able to enjoy this world, who begin with the world unseen. They alone enjoy it, who have first abstained from it. They alone can truly feast, who have first fasted; they alone are able to use the world, who have learned not to abuse it; they alone inherit it, who take it as a shadow of the world to come, and who for that world to come relinquish it.

GLORY ENDED

THE ONLY display of royal greatness, the only season of majesty, homage, and glory, which our Lord had on earth, was in His infancy and youth. Gabriel's message to Mary was in its style and manner such as befitted an Angel speaking to Christ's Mother. Elizabeth, too, saluted Mary, and the future Baptist his hidden Lord, in the same honourable way. Angels announced his birth, and the shepherds worshipped. A star appeared, and the wise men rose from the East and made Him offerings. He was brought to the temple, and Simeon took Him in His arms, and returned thanks for Him. He grew to twelve years old, and again He appeared in the temple, and took His seat in the midst of the doctors.

But here His earthly majesty had its end, or if seen afterwards, it was but now and then, by glimpses and by sudden gleams, but with no steady sustained light, and no diffused radiance. We are told at the close of the last mentioned narrative, that He went down with His parents, and came to Nazareth, *and was subject to them*. His subjection and servitude now began in fact. He had come in the form of a servant, and now He took on Him a servant's office. How much is contained in the idea of His subjection! and it began, and His time of glory ended, when He was twelve years old. "Jesus meek and humble of Heart, make our hearts like unto Thine."

He who has thrown himself out of this world, alone can overcome it; he who has cut himself loose of it, alone can be touched by it; he alone can be courageous, who does not fear it; he alone firm, who is not moved by it; he alone severe with it, who does not love it.

FOLLOW ME

OUR SAVIOUR'S words are not of a nature to be heard once and no more; to understand them we must feed upon them, as if by little and little growing into their meaning.

To follow Thee has two sides, a severe side, and a beautiful; and I shall be sure to swerve from the narrow way which leads to life, if I indulge myself in what is beautiful, while I put aside what is severe.

Thus, I know that zeal consists in a strict attention to Thy commands—a scrupulousness, vigilance, heartiness and punctuality, which bears with not reasoning or questioning about them—an intense thirst for the advancement of Thy glory—a shrinking from sin—an indignation, nay impatience, at witnessing Thy honor insulted—a quickness of feeling when Thy name is mentioned—a fullness of purpose, an heroic determination to yield Thee service at whatever sacrifice of personal feeling—an energetic resolve to push through all difficulties, were they as mountains, when Thy eye or Thy hand but give the sign—a carelessness of ob-

loquy or reproach or persecution, a forget-
fulness of all that is naturally dear to me,
when Thou dost say "Follow Me."

TENDER MERCY

WHEN THOU didst take flesh and appear on earth, Thou didst show us the
Godhead in a new manifestation. Thou
didst invest Thyself, as it were, with a new
set of attributes, those of our flesh, taking
unto Thyself a human soul and body, in
order that thoughts, feelings, affections,
might be Thine, which could respond to
ours and certify to us Thy tender mercy.

Let me go out to meet Thee with contrite and expectant heart; and though
Thou dost delay Thy coming, let me
watch for Thee in the cold and dreariness
which must one day have an end. Amen.

THY SACRED HEART

(At Lazarus' Grave)

JESUS, at Lazarus' grave, Thou didst
weep from the gentleness and mercy, the
encompassing, loving kindness and exuberant, fostering affection of the Son of God

[22]

for Thy own work, the race of man. Their tears touched Thee at once, as their miseries had brought Thee down from heaven. Thy ear was open to them, and the sound of weeping went at once to Thy Sacred Heart. "Jesus, meek and humble of heart, etc."

CONFESS THEE

BLESSED are they who give the flower of their days and their strength of soul and body to Thee.

Blessed are they who in their youth turn to Thee Who didst give Thy life for them, and wouldst fain give it to them and implant it in them, that they may live forever.

Blessed are they who resolve—come good, come evil, come sunshine, come tempest, come honor, come dishonor—that Thou shalt be their Lord and Master, their King and God! They will come to a perfect end, and to peace at the last. They will, with Jacob, confess Thee, ere they die, as the God that fed them all their life long; and with David, that in the valley of the shadow of death, they fear no evil, for Thou art with them. Thou art the Lord their God, the Holy one of Israel, their Saviour. Amen.

The day will be when I shall see Thee surrounded by Thy Holy Angels. I shall be brought into that blessed company, in which all will be pure, all bright. I come now to learn to endure Thee, the Holy One and Thy Servants. Amen.

IMMORTALITY

THE RAIN falls, and the wind blows; and showers and storms have no existence beyond the time when we felt them; they are nothing in themselves. But if we have but once seen any child of Adam, we have seen an immortal soul. It has not passed away as a breeze or sunshine, but it lives; it lives at this moment. May this thought be upon me day by day, especially when I am tempted to sin.

All of us must come to Christ, in some sense or other, through things naturally unpleasant to us. He who has really tasted of the true Cross, can taste no bitterer pain, no keener joy.

[24]

PRIVILEGES

WERE I pure as the Angels, yet in Thy sight, I could not but fear. The Seraphim veiled their faces while they cried, Glory!

I beg of Thee grace wherewith to enter into the depth of my privileges,—to enjoy what I possess—to believe in, to use, to improve, to glory in my present gifts as a member of Christ, child of God and inheritor of the kingdom of heaven. Amen.

COMFORTING

MAN is born to trouble, "as the sparks fly upward." More or less, we all have our severe trials of pain and sorrow. If we go on for some years in the world's sunshine, it is only that troubles, when they come, should fall heavier. Such at least is the general rule. Sooner or later we fare as other men; happier than they only if we learn to bear our portion more religiously; and more favoured if we fall in with those who themselves have suffered, and can aid us with their sympathy and their experience. And then, while we profit from what they can give us, we may learn from them freely to give what we have freely received, comforting in turn others with the comfort which our brethren have given us from God.

HIS BRETHREN

GOD can make the stones bread. He can feed us with every word which proceedeth from His mouth. He could, did He so will, make us calm, resigned, tender-hearted, and sympathising, without trial; but it is His will ordinarily to do so by means of trial. Even he Himself, when He came on earth, condescended to gain knowledge by experience; and what He did Himself, that He makes His brethren do. "Jesus meek and humble of heart, etc."

ROD OF GOD

AND IN like manner, when a man, in whom dwells His grace, is lying on the bed of suffering, or when he has been stripped of his friends and is solitary, he has, in a peculiar way, tasted of the powers of the world to come, and exhorts and consoles with authority. He who has been long under the rod of God, becomes God's possession. He bears in his body marks, and is sprinkled with drops, which nature could not provide for him. He "cometh from Edom, with dyed garments from Bozra," and it is easy to see with whom he has been conversing.

EVERY SERVICE

WITHOUT impatiently settling anything absolutely about our own real state in God's sight, and how it will fare with us at the last day, at least we may allow ourselves to believe that we are at present evidently blessed by being made subservient to His purposes of mercy to others; as washing the disciples' feet, and pouring into their wounds oil and wine. So we shall say to ourselves, thus far, merciful Saviour, we have attained; not to be assured of our salvation, but of our usefulness. So far we know, and enough surely for sinful man, that we are allowed to promote His glory who died for us. Taught by our own pain, our own sorrow, nay, by our own sin, we shall have hearts and minds exercised for every service of love towards those who need it. Amen.

AFTER CHRIST

WE SHALL in our measure be comforters after the image of the Almighty Paraclete, and that in all senses of the word,—advocates, assistants, soothing aids. Our words and advice, our very manner, voice, and look, will be gentle and tranquillizing, as of those who have borne their cross after Christ. We shall not pass by His little ones rudely, as the world does. The voice of the widow and the orphan, the poor and destitute, will at once reach our ears, however low they speak. Our hearts will open towards them; our word and deed befriend them. The ruder passions of man's nature, pride and anger, envy and strife, which so disorder the Christian, these will be quelled and brought under in others by the earnestness and kindness of our example.

Such too was Our Lord's forerunner,

the Holy Baptist, an austere man, cut off from among his brethren, living in the wilderness, feeding on harsh fare, yet so far removed from sternness towards those who sincerely sought the Lord, that his preaching was almost described in prophecy as the very language of consolation, "Be comforted, be comforted, my people, —speak ye to the heart of Jerusalem."

NONE BESIDES

THE CONTEMPLATION of Thee, and nothing but it, is able fully to open and relieve the mind, to unlock, occupy, and fix our affections. We may indeed love things created with great intenseness, but such affection, when disjoined from the love of the Creator, is like a stream running in a narrow channel, impetuous, vehement, turbid. The heart runs out, as it were, only at one door; it is not an expanding of the whole man. Created natures cannot open us, or elicit the ten thousand mental senses which belong to us, and through which we really live. None but the presence of our Maker can enter us; for to none besides can the whole heart

in all its thoughts and feelings be unlocked and subjected. Amen.

HEART'S MEASURE

"GOD HATH sent the Spirit of His Son
into our hearts." "He is greater than our
heart, and knoweth all things." It is this
feeling of simple and absolute confidence
and communion, which soothes and satisfies those to whom it is vouchsafed. We
know that even our nearest friends enter
into us but partially, and hold intercourse
with us only at times; whereas the consciousness of a perfect and enduring Presence, and it alone, keeps the heart open.
Withdraw the Object on which it rests,
and it will relapse again into its state of
confinement and constraint; and in proportion as it is limited, either to certain
seasons or to certain affections, the heart is
straitened and distressed.

If it be not over bold to say it, He
who is infinite can alone be our heart's
measure; He alone can answer to the mysterious assemblage of feelings and thoughts
which it has within it. "Neither is there
any creature invisible in His sight, but all
[30]

things are naked and opened to his eyes to whom our speech is."

And especially it is instanced in St. Paul, who seems to delight in the continual laying open of his heart to God, and submitting it to His scrutiny, and waiting for His Presence upon it; or, in other words, in the joy of a good conscience. With him I pray to live in all good conscience before God until His day. Amen.

WORK WITH HIM

LET ME beware of lapsing back; let me avoid temptation. Let me strive by quietness and caution to cherish the feeble flame, and shelter it from the storms of this world. God is bringing me into a higher world of self-denial; let me work with Him. Amen.

For St. Paul trials brought with them spiritual benefits; but even as he regarded this world, he (St. Paul) felt he had cause for joy and thankfulness, in spite of sorrows, pains, labors, and self-denials.

OBEYING IT

HE IS leading forward His redeemed, He is training His elect, one and all, to the one perfect knowledge and imitation of Christ; not, however, without their co-operation, but by means of calls which they are to obey, and which if they do not obey, they lose place, and fall behind in their heavenly course. He leads them forward from grace to grace, and from merit to merit, up the steps of the ladder whose top reacheth to heaven. We pass from one state of holiness to another; we are introduced into a higher region from a lower, by listening to Christ's call and obeying it. Amen.

TREMBLING

IF GOD calls us to greater renunciation of the world, and exacts a sacrifice of our hopes and fears, this is our gain, this is a mark of His love for us, this is a thing to be rejoiced in. Such thoughts, when properly entertained, have no tendency to puff us up; for if the prospect is noble, yet the risk is more fearful. While we pursue high excellence, we walk among precipices, and a fall is easy. Hence the Apostle urges us to work out our salvation "with fear and trembling."

PLEASE GOD

AGAIN the more men aim at high things, the more sensitive perception they have of their own shortcomings; and this again is adapted to humble them especially. We need not fear spiritual pride then, in following Christ's call, if we follow it as men in earnest. Earnestness has no time to compare itself with the state of other men; earnestness has too vivid a feeling of its own infirmities to be elated at itself. Earnestness is simply set on doing God's will. It simply says, "Speak, Lord, for thy servant heareth, Lord, what wilt thou have me do?" Oh that we had more of this spirit! Oh that we could take that simple view of things, as to feel that the one thing which lies before us is to please God!

LOVE AND FOLLOW

WHAT gain is it to please the world, to please the great, nay even to please those whom we love, compared with this? What gain is it to be applauded, admired, courted, followed, compared with this one aim, of not being disobedient to a heavenly vision? What can this world offer comparable with that insight into spiritual things, that keen faith, that heavenly peace, that high sanctity, that everlasting communion, that hope of glory, which they have who in sincerity love and follow our Lord Jesus Christ?

Let us beg and pray Him day by day to reveal Himself to our souls more fully; to quicken our senses; to give us sight and hearing, taste and touch of the world to come; so to work within us that we may sincerely say, "By Thy will Thou hast conducted me, and with Thy glory Thou hast received me. For what have I in heaven? and besides Thee what do I desire upon earth? For Thee my flesh and my heart hath fainted away; Thou art the God of my heart, and the God that is my portion for ever."

IN THE END

WHAT are my ventures on the truth of Thy word? How is it that I am so contented with things as they are, that I make such excuses, if anyone presses on me the necessity of something higher, the duty of bearing the Cross, if I would earn the Crown, of the Lord Jesus Christ? For "every one that hath left house for Thy name's sake shall receive an hundredfold and shall possess life everlasting."

Let me go to Thee for grace. Let me seek Thy face. Let me come where Thou givest grace. Let me come to the sacraments of grace, in which Thou givest Thy Holy Spirit, to enable me to do that which by nature I cannot do, and to be a servant of the Almighty. Amen.

If I come to Thee not seeking a sign but determined to go on seeking Thee, honoring Thee, serving Thee, trusting Thee, whether I see light, or feel comfort, or discern my growth, or no, I shall find, even while I am seeking, before I call, that Thou wilt answer me, and I shall in the end find myself saved wondrously. For shall not they that hope in the Lord renew their strength? they that walk, not faint?

THY COMING

WHAT is it to watch for Christ? He says to all: "Watch." Another warning is given elsewhere both by our Lord and by His Apostles. For instance; we have the parable of the Ten Virgins, five of whom were wise and five foolish; on whom the bridegroom, after tarrying, came suddenly, and five were found without oil. On which Our Lord says, "Watch . . . you know not the day nor the hour." Again He says, "Watch . . . praying at all times . . . that you may be accounted worthy . . . to stand before the Son of man."

In like manner He upbraided Peter thus: "Simon, sleepest Thou? couldst thou not watch one hour?" In like manner St. Paul in his epistle to the Romans, "It is now the hour for us to rise from sleep." In like manner St. Peter, "Be prudent and watch." And St. John in the Apocalypse, "Behold, I come . . . Blessed is he that watcheth." I am not simply to believe, but to watch; not simply to love, but to watch; not simply to obey, but to watch; to watch for what? For that great event, Thy coming. Amen.

COME

THOU ART behind this material frame-work; earth and sky are but a veil going between Thee and me; the day will come when Thou wilt rend this veil, and show Thyself to me. And then, according as I have waited for Thee, wilt Thou recompense me. If I have forgotten Thee, Thou wilt not know me; but blessed are those whom Thou when Thou comest shall find *watching*. Thou wilt make them sit down to meat, and passing Thou wilt minister unto them.

Thou art not far off, though Thou dost seem so, but close behind this visible screen of things which hides Thee from me.

Give me the tender and sensitive heart which hangs on the thought of Thee, Christ Jesus, and lives in Thy love. Amen.

BE RESIGNED

WELL were it for me, if I had the character of mind instanced in St. Paul; the temper of dependence upon God's providence, and thankfulness under it, and careful memory of all He has done for me. It would be well if I were in the habit of looking at all I have as God's gift, undeservedly given, and day by day continued to me solely by His mercy.

He gave; He may take away. He gave me all I have, life, health, strength, reason, enjoyment, the light of conscience; whatever I have good and holy within me; whatever of a renewed will; whatever love towards Him; whatever power over myself; whatever prospect of heaven.

He gave me relatives, friends, education, training, knowledge, the Church, the Sacraments, All comes from Him. He gave; He may take away. Did He take away, I should be called on to follow Job's pattern, and be resigned: "The Lord gave, and the Lord hath taken away. As it hath pleased the Lord, so it is done. Blessed be the name of the Lord."

HIS NAME JESUS

SINCE THOU art the All-holy Son of God, though Thou didst condescend to be born into the world, Thou necessarily didst come into it in a way suitable to the

All-holy, and different from that of other men. Thou didst take our nature upon Thee, but not our sin; taking our nature in a way above nature.

Didst Thou then come from heaven in the clouds? Didst Thou frame a body for Thyself out of the dust of the earth? No; Thou wast, as other men, "made of a woman," as St. Paul speaks, that Thou mightest take on Thee, not another nature, but the nature of man.

It had been prophesied from the beginning that the Seed of the woman should bruise the serpent's head. Two separate Angels, one to Mary, one to Joseph, declare who the adorable agent was, by whom this miracle was wrought. "Joseph, son of David, fear not to take unto thee Mary thy wife, for that which is conceived in her, is of the Holy Ghost"; and what followed from this? He proceeds, "And she shall bring forth a son: and thou shalt call His name Jesus. For He shall save His people from their sins." The Angel Gabriel had already said to Mary, "The Holy which shall be born of thee shall be called the Son of God."

IMMACULATE PURITY

THOU who art all purity came to an impure race to raise them to Thy purity. Thou, the brightness of God's glory, didst come in a body of flesh, which was pure and holy as Thyself, "not having spot or wrinkle or any such thing but that it should be holy and without blemish"; and this Thou didst for our sake, that we might be partakers of Thy holiness.

Thou art all-perfect in Thy original Divine nature, but Thou didst take upon Thyself what was ours for the sake of us to sow the seed of eternal life in our hearts and to raise us to that immaculate purity and that fullness of grace which is in Thee.

FIRST AMONG MANY

THOU, the first principle and pattern of all things, came to be the beginning and pattern of human kind, the firstborn of every creature of the whole creation. Thou, the everlasting Light, didst become the Light of men; Thou, the Life from eternity, didst become the Life of a race dead in sin; Thou, the Word of God, didst come to be a spiritual Word to save our souls; Thou, the co-equal Son of the Father, didst come to be the Son of God in our flesh that Thou mightest raise us to the adoption of sons, and might be the first among many brethren.

THEIR SYMPATHY

THOUGH I am in a body of flesh, a member of this world, I have but to kneel down reverently in prayer, and I am at once in the society of Saints and Angels. Am I under trial? I have their sympathy.

CARE OF ME

WHAT matters it what I eat, what I drink, how I am clothed, where I lodge, what is thought of me, what becomes of me, since I am not at home?

It is felt every day, even as regards this world, that when we leave home for a while we are unsettled. This, then, is the kind of feeling which a belief in Christ's coming will create within me.

It is not worth while establishing ourselves here; it is not worth while spending time and thought on such an object. I shall hardly have got settled when I shall have to move. The Lord is at hand; this is not my rest; this is not my abiding-place. I shall cast all my care upon Thee, for Thou hast care of me. May I in time, in my mode of talking and acting, in my religious observances and my daily conduct, fear Thee while I love Thee. Amen.

IN HIS BEAUTY

WHILE THOU wast here, since Thou couldst not acquiesce or pleasure Thyself in the earth, so Thou wouldst none of its vaunted goods. When Thou humbledest Thyself unto Thy own sinful creation, Thou wouldst not let that creation minister to Thee of its best, as if disdaining to receive offering or tribute from a fallen world. It is only nature regenerate which may venture to serve the Holy One. He would not accept lodging or entertainment, acknowledgement, or blandishment, from the kingdom of darkness.

Thou wouldst not be made a king; Thou wouldst not accept where Thou mightest lay Thy head. Thy life lay not in man's breath or man's smile; it was hid in Him from Whom Thou didst come and to Whom Thou didst return.

There is but one right way; it is the way in which Thou dost look at the world. May I look at it in Thy way. May I see things as Thou dost see them. May I aim to look at the life to come, and the world unseen, as Thou dost, that I may see the King in all His beauty. Amen.

THINE

LET ME beg of Thee to lead me on in Thy perfect and narrow way, and to be a lantern to my feet, and a light to my path, while I walk in it.

What is it to me how my future path lies, if it be but Thy path? What is it to me whither it leads, so that in the end it leads to Thee? What is it to me what Thou dost put upon me, so that Thou enablest me to undergo it with a pure conscience, a true heart, not desiring anything of this world in comparison of Thee? What is it to me what terror befalls me, if Thou be but at hand to protect and strengthen me?

Thou hast brought me thus far, in order to bring me further, in order to bring me on to the end. Thou wilt never leave me nor forsake me; so that I may boldly say, Thou hast redeemed me, and called me by my name: I am Thine.

I know that Thou art All-holy, yet I come before Thee; I place myself under Thy pure and piercing eyes. I know that Thou art All-merciful and that Thou so sincerely didst desire my salvation that Thou hast died for me. Amen.

LIVING WITH THY GOD

LET me labor to approve myself to Thee. If I be in a crowd, still be I as a hermit, in the wilderness. Thou wast alone, and lived alone, the immaculate Son of a Virgin Mother; and Thou didst choose the mountain summit or the garden as Thy home.

In Thy case sorrow and pain went with Thy loneliness; not, like Adam, the first hermit, eating freely of all trees but fasting in the wilderness for forty days, not tempted to eat of that one through wantonness, but urged in utter destitution of food to provide Thyself with some necessary bread,—not as a king giving names to fawning brutes, but one among the wild beasts,—not granted a helpmeet for Thy support, but praying alone in the dark morning—not dressing the herbs and flowers, but dropping blood upon the ground in agony,—not falling into a deep sleep in Thy garden, but buried there after Thy passion; yet still like the first Adam, solitary,—like the first Adam, living with Thy God and Holy Angels. "Our Father, who art in heaven, etc."

THY SOLITUDE

AND this is the more remarkable, both because Thou camest to do a great work in a short ministry, and because the same characteristic will be found in Thy servants also; nay, in Thy most laboriously employed and most successfully active servants, before and after Thee. Abraham, Isaac and Jacob were as "plain men dwelling in tents"; Moses lived for forty years a shepherd's life; and when at length he was set over the chosen people, still in one of the most critical moments of his government, he had long retirements in the Mount with God. Samuel was brought up within the Temple: Elias lived in the deserts; so did the Baptist, his antitype. Even the Apostles had their seasons of solitude. We hear of St. Peter of Joppa; and St. Paul had his labors again and again suspended by imprisonment; as if such occasional respite from exertion were as necessary for the spirit as sleep is for the body.

May then Thy solitude and that of Thy servants be my guide. I know that Thou art the true light, which enlighteneth every man that cometh into this world. Amen.

EXCEEDING JOY

IT IS written that through much tribulation we must enter into the kingdom of God. God has all things in His own hands. He can spare, He can inflict: He often spares (may He spare us still!) but He often tries us,—in one way or another He tries every one. At some time or other of the life of every one there is pain, and sorrow, and trouble. So it is; and the sooner perhaps we can look upon it as a law of our Christian condition, the better.

One generation comes, and then another. They issue forth and succeed like leaves in spring; and in all, this law is observable. They are tried, and then they triumph; they are humbled, and then are exalted; they overcome the world, and then they sit down on Christ's throne.

Hence, St. Peter, who at first was in such amazement and trouble at his Lord's afflictions, bids us not look on suffering as a strange thing, as though some strange thing happened to us, but rejoice, inasmuch as we are partakers of the sufferings of Christ, as also partakers of that glory which is to be revealed in time to come. Amen.

THE THOUGHT OF GOD

WE MUST take up the cross of Christ, that we may wear His crown. Give our hearts to Him, and we shall for ourselves solve the difficulty, how Christians can be sorrowful, yet always rejoicing. We shall find that lightness of heart and cheerfulness are quite consistent with that new and heavenly character which He gives us, though to gain it in any good measure, we must for a time be sorrowful, and ever after thoughtful. But He gives us fair warning, we must at first take His word on trust; and if we do not, there is no help for it. He says, "Come unto Me, . . . and I will refresh you." We must begin on faith. We cannot see at first whither He is leading us, and how light will rise out of the darkness.

We must begin by denying ourselves our natural wishes,—a painful work; by refraining from sin, by rousing from sloth, by preserving our tongue from insincere words, and our hands from deceitful dealings, and our eyes from beholding vanity; by watching against the first rising of anger, pride, impurity, obstinacy, jealousy; by learning to endure the laugh of irreligious men for Christ's sake; by forcing our minds to follow seriously the words of prayer, though it be difficult to us, and by keeping before us the thought of God all through the day.

These things we shall be able to do if we do but seek the mighty help of God the Holy Spirit which is given to us.

IN THY LOVE

I PRAY Thee to give me the heart to seek Thee in sincerity. I pray Thee to make me in earnest. I have one work only, to bear my cross after Thee. I resolve in Thy strength to do so. I pray Thee to give me what Scripture calls an honest and good heart, or, a perfect heart, and, without waiting, I will begin at once to obey Thee with the best heart I have. I have to seek Thy face; obedience is the only way of seeking Thee. All my duties are acts of obedience. To do what Thou dost bid is to obey Thee, and to obey Thee is to approach Thee.

Let me not give over my attempts to serve God, though I see nothing come of them. Let me watch and pray, and obey my conscience, though I cannot perceive my own progress in holiness. Let me go on. I cannot but go forward; believe it, though I do not see it. Do the duties of my calling, though they are distasteful to me.

May I, then, always grow in heavenly knowledge, and, with that end, labour to improve what is already given me, be it more or be it less, knowing that he that is faithful in little things is faithful also in many, and that to him that hath, more shall be given. Amen.

ALL CHRISTIANS

ONE person is a king and rules, another is a subject and obeys; but if both are Christians, both have in common a gift so great, that in the sight of it, the difference between ruling and obeying is as nothing. All Christians are kings in God's sight; they are kings in His unseen kingdom, in His spiritual world, in the Communion of Saints. They seem like other men, but they have crowns on their heads, and glorious robes around them, and Angels to wait on them, though our bodily eyes see it not. Such are all Christians, high and low; all Christians who remain in that state in which Baptism and Penance place them.

God did not wait till I should do some good thing before He blessed me. No! He knew I could do no good thing of myself. So He came to me first; He loved me before I loved Him; He gave me a work which He first made me able to do. He placed me in a new and heavenly state, in which, while I remain, I am safe. "Thy will be done."

MEEK AND HUMBLE

OUR LORD'S character is described as meekness and lowliness; for we are told to "learn" of Him who was "meek and humble of heart." The same character is presented to us at greater length in our Saviour's sermon on the Mount in which seven notes of a Christian are given to us, in themselves of a painful and humbling character, but joyful, because they are blessed by Him. He mentions, first, "the poor in Spirit"; this is denoted in Scripture under the word "humble of heart"— secondly, those "that mourn"; and this surely is their peculiarity who are bearing on their shoulders the yoke of Christ;— thirdly, "the meek"; and these too are spoken of in the gospel when He bids us to be like Himself who "is meek";— fourthly, those who "hunger and thirst after justice"; and what justice, but that which Christ's Cross wrought out, and which becomes our justice when we take on us the yoke of the Cross? Fifthly, "the merciful"; and as the Cross is in itself the work of infinite mercy, so when we bear it, it makes us merciful. Sixthly, "the pure in heart"; and this is the very benefit which the Cross first does to us when marked on our forehead when infants, to sever us from the world, the flesh, and the devil, to circumcise us from the first Adam, and to make us pure as He is pure. Seventhly, "the peace-makers," and as He made peace by the blood of His Cross, so do we become peace-makers after His pattern. And, lastly, after all seven, He adds, those "who are persecuted for justice sake"; which is nothing but the Cross itself, and the truest form of His yoke, spoken of last of all, after mention has been made of its fruits. "Jesus, meek and humble of heart, etc."

HIS CHARACTER

WE KNOW what Our Lord's character was; how grave and subdued His speech, His manner, His acts; what calmness, self-possession, tenderness, and endurance; how He resisted evil; how He turned His cheek to the smiter; how He blessed when persecuted; how He resigned Himself to His God and Father, how He suffered silently, and opened not His mouth, when accused maliciously. "Jesus, meek and humble of heart, etc."

AGAINST HIM

LET me not deceive myself; there are not two ways of salvation—a broad and a narrow. The world, which chooses the broad way, in consequence hates and spurns the narrow way; and in turn our Blessed Lord, who has chosen for me the narrow way, hates, scorns, spurns, denounces, the broad way. Surely He does so; He hates the broad way as entirely as the world hates the narrow way; and if I am persuaded to take part with the world, I take part against Him. When St. Peter said, "Be it far from Thee, Lord," being shocked at the notice that his Lord should suffer, what was His answer? Did He thank him for his zeal? Did He, at least, let it pass in silence? He answered, "Go behind Me, Satan, thou art a scandal unto Me; because thou savorest not the things that are of God, but that are of men."

THUS we too are bidden lend and give, asking for nothing again; revenge not ourselves; give our cloak when our coat is taken; offer the left cheek when the right is smitten; suffer without complaint; account persons better than they are; keep from bitter words; pray when others would be impatient to act; deny ourselves for the sake of others; live contented with what we are; preserve an ignorance of sin and of the world; what is all this, but a character of mind which the world scorns and ridicules even more than it hates?

The meek and humble are despised by the world, but they have subdued the world. Nay, though they seem most unmanly, they in the event have proved most heroic. For the heroical character springs out of them. He who has thrown himself out of this world, alone can overcome it; he who has cut himself loose of it, alone cannot be touched by it; he alone can be courageous, who does not fear it; he alone firm, who is not moved by it; he alone severe with it, who does not love it. He who has nothing to hope from the world, has nothing to fear from it. He who has really tasted of the true Cross, can taste no bitterer pain, no keener joy. "Because by Thy holy cross, Thou hast redeemed the world."

HIS GRACE

WHEN we felt how necessary it was to serve God, but felt keenly the power of temptation; when we acknowledged in our hearts that God was holy and most adorable, and obedience to His will most lovely and admirable, and yet recollected instances of our past disobedience, and feared lest all our renewed resolutions to serve Him would be broken and swept away by the old Adam as mercilessly as heretofore, and that Satan would regain us, and yet prayed earnestly to God for His saving help; then He saved us against our fear, surprising us by the strength of His grace.

GREAT CAPTAIN

THIS many a one must recollect in his own case. It happens to Christians not once, but again and again through life. Troubles are lightened, trials are surmounted, fears disappear. We are enabled to do things above our strength by trusting in Christ; we overcome our most innocent wishes; we conquer ourselves; we make a way through the powers of the world, the flesh, and the devil; the waves divide, and our Lord, the great Captain of our salvation, leads us over. "Glory be to the Father, etc."

Religion has a store of wonderful secrets which no one can communicate to another, and which are most pleasant and delightful to know. "Call on Me," says God by the prophet, "and I will answer thee, and show thee great and mighty things which thou knowest not of." This is no mere idle boast, but a fact which all who seek God will find to be true, though they cannot perhaps clearly express their meaning.

Strange truths about ourselves, about God, about our duty, about the world, about heaven and hell, new modes of viewing things, discoveries which cannot be put into words, marvellous prospects and thoughts half understood, deep convictions inspiring joy and peace, these are a part of the revelation which Christ, the Son of God, brings to those who obey Him. Moses had much toil to gain from the great God—some scattered rays of the truth, and that for his personal comfort, not for all Israel; but Christ has brought from His Father for all of us the full and perfect way of life.

Grant me the grace of this truth, of this mercy, of the gift of true wisdom in its fullness. Amen.

A SHARE

ST. PETER makes it almost a description of a Christian, that he loves Him whom he has not seen; speaking of Christ, he says, "Whom having not seen, you love: in Whom also now, though you see Him not, you believe and believing shall rejoice with joy unspeakable and glorified." Again he speaks of "tasting" that the Lord is sweet. Unless we have a true love of Christ, we are not His true disciples; and we cannot love Him unless we have heartfelt gratitude to Him; and we cannot duly feel gratitude, unless we feel keenly what He suffered for us. It seems impossible, under the circumstances of the case, that any one can have attained to the love of Christ, who feels no distress, no misery, at the thought of His bitter pains, and no self-reproach at having through his own sins had a share in causing them. "My God, I am sorry."

FORGIVENESS

RATHER than Israel should forfeit the promised land, Moses offered to give up his own portion in it, and the exchange was accepted. He was excluded, dying in sight, not in enjoyment of Canaan, while the people went in under Joshua. This was a figure of Him that was to come. Our Saviour Christ died, that we might live: He consented to lose the light of God's countenance, that we might gain it. By His cross and passion, He made atonement for our sins, and bought for us the forgiveness of God. "We adore Thee, O Christ, and bless Thee, etc."

[58]

HIS GLORY

IS HE habitually in my thoughts? Do I think of Him, and of His Son our Saviour, through the day? When I eat and drink, do I thank Him, not as a mere matter of form, but in spirit? When I do things in themselves right, do I lift up my mind to Him, acting ever conscientiously, desiring to know His will more exactly than I do at present, and aiming at fulfilling it more completely and abundantly? Do I wait on His grace to enlighten, renew, strengthen me?

May there be no barrier, no cloud, no earthly object, interposed between my soul and my Saviour and Redeemer. May Christ be in my heart, and therefore all that comes from my heart, my thoughts, words, and actions, may all savour of Christ. The Lord be my light, and may I shine with His illumination. Amen.

To take up our cross, is to take upon us His yoke; and though He calls it an easy yoke, yet it is easy because it is His yoke and He makes it easy; still it does not cease to be a yoke, and it is troublesome and distressing, because it is a yoke.

GLORIOUS MYSTERIES

(*A Meditation*)

AT CHRISTMAS we joy with the natural, unmixed joy of children, but at Easter our joy is highly wrought and refined in its character. It is not the spontaneous and unartificial outbreak which the news of Redemption might occasion, but it is thoughtful; it has a long history before it, and has run through a long course of feelings before it becomes what it is. It is a last feeling and not a first.

St. Paul describes its nature and its formation, when he says, "We glory also in tribulations, knowing that tribulation worketh patience; and patience trial; and trial hope; and hope confoundeth not, because the charity of God is poured forth in our hearts by the Holy Ghost, who is given to us."

Or as it was fulfilled in the case of our Lord Himself, who, as being the Captain of our salvation, was made perfect through sufferings. Accordingly, Christmas Day is ushered in with a time of awful expectation only, but Easter Day with the long fast of Lent, and the rigors of the Holy

Week just past; and it springs out and (as it were) is born of Good Friday.

And therefore now, though it is over, I cannot so shake off at once what has been, as to enter fully into what is. Risen Christ, though Thou didst suffer and die, yet didst rise again vigorously on the third day, having loosed the pains of death, I cannot accomplish in my contemplation of Thee, what Thou didst accomplish really; for Thou art the Holy One, and I am a sinner. I have the languor and oppression of my old self upon me, though I be new; and therefore I must beg Thee who art the Prince of Life, the Life itself, to carry me forth into Thy new world, for I cannot walk thither, and seat me down whence, like Moses, I may see the land, and meditate upon its beauty!

None rejoice in Easter-tide less than those who have not grieved in Lent. Feast-day and fast-day, holy tide and other tide, are one and the same to them. Hence they do not realize the other world at all. My Saviour says, "Blessed are they that mourn: for they shall be comforted," and what is true hereafter, is true here.

I must make my Saviour's life and

death ever present to me: I must transport myself back to the time of Thy sojourn on earth. I must act over again and celebrate Thy history, in my own observance. I must form my estimate of things upon it; I must hold it as a practical principle in my heart. Make me sure that as previous humiliation sobers my joy, it alone secures them to me. In this does Christian mirth differ from worldly, that it is subdued; and how shall it be subdued except that the past keeps its hold upon us, and while it warns and sobers me, actually indisposes and tames my flesh against indulgence? Providential affliction brings my soul nearer to Thee.

The poor shall be rich, the lowly shall be exalted, those that sow in tears shall reap in joy, those that mourn shall be comforted, those that suffer with Christ shall reign with Him. Easter is preceded by humiliation that we may keep it in a refined, subdued, chastised spirit, which is the true rejoicing in the Lord.

Whether I read the account of St. Mary Magdalen weeping at the sepulchre, seeing Jesus and knowing Him not, recognising His voice, attempting to embrace His feet, and then sinking into silent awe and delight, till she rose and hastened to tell the perplexed Apostles;—or turn to that solemn meeting which was the third, when He stood on the shore and addressed His disciples, and Peter plunged into the water, and then with the rest was awed in silence and durst not speak, but obeyed His command, and ate of the fish in silence, and so remained in the presence of One in whom they joyed, whom they loved, as He knew, more than all things, till He broke silence by asking Peter if he loved Him:—or lastly, consider the time when He appeared unto a great number of disciples on the mountain in Galilee and all worshipped Him:—do I not see that their Easter was such a holy, tender, reverent, manly joy, not so tender as to be effeminate, but (as if) an Angel's mood, the mingled offering of all that is best and highest in man's and woman's nature brought together, St. Mary Magdalen and St. Peter blended into St. John?

And here perhaps we learn a lesson from the seeming silence which scripture observes concerning the Blessed Virgin after the Resurrection; as if she, who was too pure and holy a flower to be more than seen here on earth, even during the season of her Son's humiliation, was altogether drawn by the Angels within the veil of the Resurrection, and had her joy in Paradise with Gabriel who had been the first to honor her, and with those elder Saints who arose after the Resurrection, appeared in the Holy City, and then vanished away.

Christ is risen; He is risen from the dead. We may well cry out, Alleluia, for the Lord Omnipotent reigneth. He has crushed all the power of the enemy under His feet. He has gone upon the lion and the adder. He has stopped the lion's mouth for us His people, and has bruised the serpent's head. There is nothing impossible to me now, if I do but enter into the fullness of my privileges, the wondrous power of my gifts.

The thing cannot be named in heaven or earth within the limits of truth and obedience which I cannot do through Christ; the petition cannot be named which may not be accorded to me for His Name's sake. For, I who have risen with Him from the grave, stand in His sight, and am allowed to use His weapons.

His infinite influence with the Father

is mine, not always to use, for perhaps in this or that effort I make, or petition I prefer, it would not be good for me; but so far mine, so fully mine, that when I ask and do things according to His will, I am really possessed of a power with God, and do prevail:—so that little as I may know when and when not, I am continually possessed of heavenly weapons, I am continually touching the springs of the most wonderful providences in heaven and earth; and by the Name, and the Sign, and the Blood of the Son of God, I am able to make the devils tremble and the Saints to rejoice.

This then be my spirit on Easter. God rested from His labors on the seventh day, yet He worketh evermore. Christ entered into His rest, yet He too ever works. I too, if it may be said, in adoring and lowly imitation of what is infinite, while I rest in Christ and rejoice in His shadow, let me too beware of sloth and cowardice, and fears; that I may be truly His in my heart, as I was made His by Baptism,—as I am made His continually, by the recurring celebration of His purifying Fasts and holy Feasts. Amen.

OUR MEASURE

WHAT a time must that forty days have been, during which, while He taught them, all His past teaching must have risen in their minds, and sent their past thoughts in overpowering contrast to their thoughts now. His manner of life, His ministry, His discourses, His parables, His miracles, His meekness, gravity, incomprehensible majesty, the mystery of His grief and joy; the agony, the scourge, the cross, the crown of thorns, the spear, the tomb; their despair, their unbelief, their perplexity, their amazement, their sudden transport, their triumph,—all this was in their minds; and surely not the least at that awful hour, when He led His breathless followers out to Bethany, on the fortieth day.

"He led them out as far as to Bethania; and lifting up His hands, He blessed them. And it came to pass, whilst He blessed them, He departed from them and was carried up to heaven." Surely all His history, all His dealings with them, came before them, gathered up in that moment. Then, as they gazed upon that dread

Divine countenance and that heavenly form, every thought and feeling which they ever had had about Him came upon them at once. He had gone through His work; theirs was to come, their work and their sufferings. He was leaving them just at the most critical time.

When Elias went up, Eliseus said: "My father, my father, the chariot of Israel and the driver thereof." With a like feeling, might the Apostles now gaze up into heaven, as if with the hope of arresting His ascent. Their Lord and their God, the light of their eyes, the stay of their hearts, the guide of their feet, was taken away. Their beloved had withdrawn Himself and was gone. Their soul failed when He spake; they sought Him but could not find Him; they called Him, but He gave them no answer. Well might they beseech Him, "leave us not orphans."

O Thou who wast so gentle and familiar with us, who didst converse with us by the way, and sit at meat with us, and didst enter the vessel with us, and teach us on the Mount, and bear the malice of the Pharisees, and feast with Martha, and raise Lazarus, art Thou gone, and shall we see Thee no more? Yet so it was determined: privileges they were to have, but not the same; and their thoughts henceforth were to be of another kind than heretofore. It was in vain wishing back what was past and over. They were but told, as they gazed, "This Jesus who is taken up from you into heaven, shall so come, as you have seen Him going into heaven."

Such are some of the feelings which the Apostles may have experienced on our Lord's Ascension; but these are after all but human and ordinary, and of a kind which all of us can enter into; but other than these were sovereign with them at that solemn time, for upon the glorious Ascension of their Lord, "they adoring" says the text, "went back into Jerusalem with great joy. And they were always in the temple, praising and blessing God." Now how was it, that when nature would have wept, the Apostles rejoiced.

When Mary came to the sepulchre and found not our Lord's body, she stood at the sepulchre weeping, and the Angels said unto her, as Christ said after them, "Woman, why weepest Thou?" Yet, on our Saviour's departure forty days afterwards, when the Angels would reprove the Apostles, they did but say, "why stand you looking up into heaven?" There was no sorrow in the Apostles, in spite of their loss, in spite of the prospect before them, but "great joy," and continual praise and blessing. May we venture to surmise that this rejoicing was the high temper of the brave and noble-minded, who have faced danger in idea and are prepared for it?

Moses brought out of Egypt a timid nation, and in the space of forty years trained it to be full of valour for the task of conquering the promised land; Christ in forty days trains His Apostles to be bold and patient instead of cowards. They mourned and wept at the beginning of the season, but at the end they are full of courage for the good fight; their spirits mount high with their Lord, and when He is received out of their sight, and their own trial begins, they return to "Jerusalem with great joy. And they were always in the temple, praising and blessing God."

Christ surely had taught them what it was to have their treasure in heaven; and they rejoiced, not that their Lord was gone, but that their hearts had gone with Him. Their hearts were no longer on earth, they were risen aloft. When He died on the Cross, they knew not whither He was gone. Before He was seized, they had asked Him, whither goest Thou? "Lord, we know not whither Thou goest?" They could but follow Him to the grave and there mourn, for they knew no better; but now they saw Him ascend on high, and in spirit they ascended with Him. Mary wept at the grave because she thought enemies had taken Him away, and she knew not where they had laid Him. "Where thy treasure is, there is thy heart also." Mary had no heart left to her, for her treasure was lost; but the Apostles were continually in the Temple, praising and blessing God, for their hearts were in heaven, or, as St. Paul says they were dead, and their "life was hid with Christ in God."

Strengthened, then, with this knowledge they were able to face those trials which Christ had first undergone Himself, and had foretold as their portion. "Whither I go," He had said to St. Peter, "thou canst not follow Me now, but thou shalt follow hereafter." And He told them, "They will put you out of the synagogues, yea, the hour cometh, that whosoever killeth you will think that he doeth service to God." That time was now coming, and they were able to rejoice in what so troubled them forty days before. For they understood the promise, "To him that shall overcome, I will give to sit with Me in My throne, as I also have overcome, and am set down with My Father in His Throne."

It will be well if we take this lesson to ourselves, and learn that great truth which the Apostles shrank from at first, but at length rejoiced in. Christ suffered, and entered into joy; so did they, in their measure, after Him. And in our measure, so do we. "Our Father, who art in heaven."

GUIDE AND TEACHER

WHEN OUR LORD was leaving His Apostles, and they were sorrowful, He consoled them by the promise of another Guide and Teacher, the Third Person in the Ever-blessed Trinity, the Holy Ghost. Accordingly, though it was expedient that the Son should go away, in order that the Comforter might come, we do not lose sight of the Son in the presence of the Comforter. On the contrary, Christ expressly announced to the Apostles concerning Him, "He shall glorify Me." Thou are present when Thou dost seem leaving Thy own to desolateness and orphanhood.

Thy presence, now that it is invisible, brings with it a host of high and mysterious feelings, such as nothing else can inspire. The thought of Thee, absent yet present, is like that of a friend taken from us, but, as it were, in dream returned to us, though, in this case, not in dream, but in reality and truth. When Thou wast going away, Thou didst say to Thy disciples, "I will see you again, and your heart shall rejoice." We believe that Thou art here, yet away,—art present, though invisible. It is a feeling of awe, wonder, and praise, which cannot be more suitably expressed than in holy Job's words, though he spoke in grief, and not as being possessed of a blessing: "Therefore I am troubled at His presence, when I consider Him I am made pensive with fear." But I will watch for Thee. Amen.

HOLY GHOST

CHRIST exercised His prophetical office in teaching, and in foretelling the future; —in His sermon on the Mount, in His parables, in His prophecy of the destruction of Jerusalem. He performed the Priest's service when He died on the Cross, as a sacrifice; and when He consecrated the bread and the wine to be a renewal of that sacrifice; and now that He intercedes for us at the right hand of God. And He showed Himself as a conqueror and a king, in rising from the dead, in ascending into heaven, in sending down the Holy Ghost to convert the nations, to receive and to rule them. "Come, O Holy Ghost."

Let us not be content with ourselves; let us not make our own hearts our home, or this world our home, or our friends our home; let us look out for a better country, that is, a heavenly. Let us look out for Him who alone can guide us to that better country; let us call heaven our home.

WATCHING FOR CHRIST

I WATCH for Thee if I have a sensitive, eager, apprehensive mind; if I am awake, alive, quick-sighted, zealous in seeking and honoring Thee; if I look out for Thee in all that happens, and if I should not be surprised, if I should not be over-agitated or overwhelmed, if I found that Thou wert coming at once.

Do I not know the feelings in matters of this life, of expecting a friend, expecting him to come, and he delays? Do I not know what it is to be in anxiety lest something should happen which may happen or may not, or to be in suspense about some important event, which makes my heart beat when I am reminded of it, and of which I think the first thing in the morning?

Do I not know what it is to have a friend in a distant country, to expect news of him, and to wonder from day to day what he is now doing, and whether he is well?

To watch for Christ is a feeling such as all these; as far as feelings of this world are fit to shadow out those of another.

AWAKE with this season to meet your God, who now summons you from His cross and tomb. Put aside the sin that doth so easily beset you, and be ye holy even as He is holy. Stand ready to suffer with Him should it be needful, that you may rise again together with Him. He can make bitter things sweet to you, and hard ways easy, if you have but the heart to desire Him to do so. He can give you Himself. He has done this for many in time past. He does it for many at all times.

Why should He not do it for me? Why should I be left out? Why should I not enter into His rest? Why should I not see His glory? O, let me not be blotted out from His book! Let me consider what a different man St. Paul was after his conversion and before,—raging like some wild beast, with persecuting fury against the Church, before Christ appeared to him, and meekly suffering persecution and glorying in it afterwards. Think of St. Peter denying Christ before the resurrection, and confessing, suffering, and dying for Him afterwards.

What need have I to humble myself; to pray God not to leave me, though I have left Him; to pray Him to give me back what I have lost, to receive a repentant prodigal, to renew in me a right heart and give me a determined will, and to enable me to follow Him perseveringly in His narrow and humbling way. Amen.

FULL OF THEE

THE PLEASURES of holiness are far more pleasant to the holy, than the pleasures of sin to the sinner. O that I could get myself to believe this! O that I had a heart to feel it and know it! O that I had a heart to taste God's pleasures and to make proof of them; to taste and see how sweet the Lord is!

Prayer was a characteristic of Christians as described in Scripture. They knew not what hour their Lord would come, and therefore they watched and prayed every hour lest they should enter into temptation. "They were always in the temple, praising and blessing God."

Thou comest to me at Holy Mass. Let me at Holy Communion approach Thee with awe and love, in Whom resides all perfection, and from Whom I am allowed to gain it. Let me come to the Sanctifier to be sanctified. Let me come to Thee to learn my duty, and to receive grace to do it. At other times of the day I am reminded of watching, toiling, struggling, and suffering; but at this moment I am reminded simply of Thy gifts towards me a sinner.

I am reminded that I can do nothing, and that Thou dost everything. This is especially the moment of grace. I come to see and to experience Thy mercies. I come before Thee as the helpless beings during Thy ministry, who were brought on beds and couches for a cure. I come to be made whole.

I come as little children to be fed and taught, as newborn babes, desiring the rational milk, that thereby I may grow unto salvation. This is a time for innocence and purity and gentleness and mildness and contentment and peace. As at Christmas, it is a time in which the Church seems decked in white, in her baptismal robe, in the bright and glistening raiment of the Holy Mount.

Thou comest at other times of the day with garments dyed in blood; but now Thou comest to me in all serenity and peace and Thou biddest me rejoice in Thee, and to love all others. With the Apostle let me put on the Lord Jesus Christ.

May each Holy Communion as it comes, find me more and more like Thee (who at these times becomest a little child for my sake) more simple-minded, more humble, more holy, more affectionate, more resigned, more happy, more full of Thee. Amen.

OUR LADY'S FAITH

"BUT MARY kept all these words, pondering them in her heart." Little is told us in Scripture concerning the Blessed Virgin, but there is one grace of which the Evangelists make her the pattern in a few simple sentences—of Faith. Zacharias questioned the Angel's message, but Mary said, "Behold the handmaid of the Lord; be it done to me according to thy word." Accordingly Elizabeth, speaking with an apparent allusion to the contrast thus ex-

hibited between her and the highly-fa-
voured Virgin Mary, said, on receiving
her salutation, "Blessed art thou among
women, and blessed is the fruit of thy
womb. Blessed art thou that believed, because those things shall be accomplished
that were spoken to thee by the Lord."

THESE WORDS

BUT MARY'S faith did not end in a mere
acquiescence in Divine providences and
revelations: as the text informs us, she
pondered them. When the shepherds
came, and told of the vision of Angels
which they had seen at the time of the
Nativity, and how one of them announced
that the Infant in her arms was the "Saviour, who is Christ the Lord," while
others did but wonder, "Mary kept all
these words pondering them in her heart."

IN HER HEART

AGAIN, when her Son and Saviour had
come to the age of twelve years, and had
left her for awhile for His Father's service,
and had been found, to her surprise, in

the Temple, amid the doctors, both hearing them and asking them questions, and had, on her addressing Him, vouchsafed to justify His conduct, we are told, "His mother kept all these words in her heart." And accordingly, at the marriage-feast in Cana, her faith anticipated his first miracle, and she said to the servants, "Whatsoever He shall say to you, do ye."

SEAT OF WISDOM

THUS, Our Lady is our pattern of Faith, both in the reception and in the study of Divine Truth. She does not think it enough to accept, she dwells upon it; not enough to possess, she uses it; she reasons upon it; not indeed reasoning first, and believing afterwards, with Zacharias; yet first believing without reasoning, next from love and reverence, reasoning after believing. And thus she symbolizes to us, not only the faith of the unlearned, but of the doctors of the Church also, who have to investigate, and weigh, and define, as well as profess the Gospel; to draw the line between truth and heresy, to anticipate or remedy the various aberrations of wrong reason; to combat pride and reck-lessness with their own arms; and thus to triumph over the sophist and the innova-tor. Seat of Wisdom, pray for us.

THEIR QUEEN

I KNOW that God's Angels are about the earth. I know that once they were even used to come in human shape. Queen of Angels, pray for us.

COMMUNION OF SAINTS

OUR SAVIOUR said, that even the lilies of the field were more gloriously arrayed than Solomon; for the lily is a living thing, the work of God; and all the glories of a king, his purple robe, and his jewelled crown, all this is but the dead work of man. But if this be true, even of God's lower works, what shall be said of His higher? If even the lilies of the field, which are cut down and cast into the oven, are more glorious than this world's great-est glory, what shall be said of God's no-bler works in the soul of man? What shall be said of the dispensation of the Spirit which "excelleth in glory?"; of that new creation of the soul, whereby He makes us His children, who by birth were children of Adam, and slaves of the devil, gives us a new and heavenly nature, implants His holy Spirit within us, and washes away all our sins?

I believe in the Holy Ghost . . . the forgiveness of sin, the resurrection of the body and life everlasting. Amen.

HEAVENLY GLORY

THIS IS the portion of the Christian, high or low; and all the glories of this world fade away before it; king and subject, man of war and keeper of the sheep, are all on a level in the kingdom of Christ; for they one and all receive those far exceeding and eternal blessings, which make this world's distinctions, though they remain distinctions just as before, yet so little, so unimportant, in comparison of heavenly glory that it is not worth while thinking about them.

May God grant, that I may improve my gifts, and trade and make merchandise with them. So that, when He cometh to reckon with me, I may be accepted! Amen.

GOD hath chosen all of us to salvation, not for our worth but for His great mercies.

David was the son of a Bethlehemite, one among the families of Israel, with nothing apparently to recommend him to God; the youngest of his brethren, and despised by them. He was sent to feed the sheep; and his father, though doubtless he loved him dearly, yet seems to have thought little of him. For when Samuel came to Jesse at God's command, in order to choose one of his sons from the rest as God might direct him, Jesse did not bring David before him, though he did bring all his other children.

David was a shepherd. The Angel appeared to the shepherds as they kept watch over their sheep at night. The most solitary, the most unlearned, God hears, God looks upon, God visits, God blesses, God brings to glory, if he is but "rich in faith." Many of you are not great in this world, my brethren, many of you are poor; but the greatest king upon earth, even Solomon in all his glory, might well exchange places with you, if you are God's children; for then you are greater than the greatest of kings.

"And David prevailed over the Philistine, with a sling and a stone."

These words declare the victory which David, the man after God's own heart, gained over Goliath, who came out of the army of the Philistines to defy the Living God; and they declare the manner of his gaining it. He gained it with a sling and with a stone; that is, by means, which to man might seem weak and hopeless, but which God Almighty blessed and prospered.

Let no one think the history of David's calling, and his victory over Goliath, of little importance to himself; it raises the mind of the Christian to God, shows us His power, and reminds us of the wonderful deliverances with which He visits His Church in every age; but besides all this, this history is useful to us Christians, as setting before us our own calling, and our conflict with the world, the flesh, and the devil.

God chose him, whose occupation was that of a shepherd; for He chooses not the great men of the world. He passes by the rich and noble; He chooses "the poor in this world, rich in faith, and heirs of the kingdom which He hath promised to them that love Him," as St. James says. Yet God took him from the sheepfolds to make him His servant and His friend. Now this is fulfilled in the case of all Christians. We are by nature poor, and mean, and nothing worth; but God chooses us and brings us near unto Himself.

THROUGH LIFE

THE DEVIL is our Goliath: we have to fight Satan, who is far more fearful and powerful than ten thousand giants, and who would to a certainty destroy us were not God with us; but praised be His name, He is with us. "Greater is He that is in you, than he that is in the world." David was first anointed with God's Holy Spirit, and then, after a while, brought forward to fight Goliath. We too are first baptized, and then brought forward to fight the devil. By degrees our work comes upon us; as children we have to fight with him a little; as time goes on, the fight opens; and at length we have our great enemy marching against us with sword and spear, as Goliath came against David. And when this war has once begun, it lasts through life. "Give us this day our daily bread."

GOD'S WILL

WHAT THEN ought we to do, when thus assailed? How must we behave when the devil comes against us? He has many ways of attack; sometimes he comes openly, sometimes craftily, sometimes he tempts us, sometimes he frightens us, but whether he comes in a pleasing or a frightful form, be sure, if we saw him himself with our eyes, he would always be hateful, monstrous, and abominable. Therefore he keeps himself out of sight. But we may be sure he is all this; and, as believing it, take the whole armour of God, that we may be able to stand in the evil day, and having done all, to stand. Quit ourselves like men, be strong. Be like David, very courageous to do God's will.

Our weapons are all-simple, yet all-powerful. The Lord's Prayer is one such weapon; when we are tempted to sin, let us turn away, kneel down seriously and solemnly, and say to God that prayer which the Lord taught us. The Creed is another weapon, equally powerful, through God's grace, equally contemptible in the eyes of the world. One or two holy texts, such as our Saviour used when He was tempted by the devil, is another weapon for our need.

Think what would have happened had David played the coward, and refused to obey God's inward voice stirring him up to fight Goliath. He would have lost his calling, he would have been tried, and have failed.

God grant us grace to use the arms which He gives us; not to neglect them, not to take arms of our own! God grant us to use His arms, and to conquer!

CHOSEN US

IF WE are living in His faith and fear, we are kings—kings in God's unseen and spiritual kingdom; and that, though like David, we are but keeping sheep, or driving cattle, or, again, working with our hands, or serving in a family, or at any other lowly labour. God seeth not as man seeth; He hath chosen us. Amen.

CONSECRATED SUFFERING

ST. PAUL was consecrated by suffering to be an Apostle of Christ; by fastings, by chastisements, by self-denials for his brethren's sake, by his forlorn, solitary life, thus did he fill up day by day those intervals of respite which the fury of his persecutors permitted.

He was beaten, he was scourged, he was chased to and fro, he was imprisoned, he was shipwrecked, he was in this life of all men most miserable, that he might understand how poor a thing mortal life is, and might learn to contemplate and describe fitly the glories of the life immortal.

Such wast thou, great Apostle St. Paul, the Apostle of comfort. Yet thou didst reveal to us: "I chastise my body, and bring it into subjection: lest perhaps, when I have preached to others, I myself should become a castaway." St. Paul, pray for us.

ST. PAUL'S CHARITY

ST. PAUL gives a great number of properties to Charity, all distinct and special. It is a name for all at once. It is patient, it is kind, it has no envy, no self-importance, no ostentation, no indecorum, no selfishness, no irritability, no malevolence. It is the fulfilling of the law. It was Charity which brought Christ down. Charity is but another name for the Comforter.

It is eternal Charity which is the bond of all things in heaven and earth; it is Charity wherein the Father and the Son are one in the unity of the Spirit; by which the Angels in heaven are one, by which all Saints are one with God, by which the Church is one upon earth.

May we be civil and obliging, kind and friendly; not envious or jealous, not quarrelsome, not spiteful or resentful, not selfish, not covetous, not niggardly, not lovers of the world, not afraid of the world, not afraid of what man can do against us.

Grant us St. Paul's Charity, for without it, we are nothing. Amen.

EVERY SOUL

MUCH INTERCOURSE with the world, has a tendency to draw off the mind from God, and deaden it to the force of religious motives and considerations. There is want of sympathy between much business and calm devotion, great splendour and a simple faith. To maintain a religious spirit in the midst of engagements and excitements of this world, though our business be one of a charitable and religious nature, is difficult. We are likely to be deceived from the very circumstance that our employments are religious. They will engross us and continually tempt us to be inattentive to the means, and to the spirit in which we pursue it. Our Lord alludes to the danger of multiplied occupations in the Parable of the Sower: "He that received the seed among thorns, is he that heareth the word, and the care of this world and the deceitfulness of riches choketh up the word, and he becometh fruitless."

HUMBLE TEMPER

OR WHEN a man feels himself possessed of good abilities; of quickness in entering into a subject, or of powers of argument to discourse readily upon it or of acuteness to detect fallacies in dispute with little effort, or of a delicate and cultivated taste, so as to separate with precision the correct and beautiful in thought and feeling from the faulty and irregular, how will such a one be tempted to self-complacency and self-approbation! How apt will he be to rely upon himself, to rest contented with himself; to be harsh and impetuous; or supercilious; or to be fastidious, indolent, unpractical; and to despise a pure, self-denying, humble temper as something irrational, dull, or needlessly rigorous!

Even the best men require some pain or grief to sober them and keep their hearts right. Thus to take the example of St. Paul himself, even his labours, sufferings, and anxieties, he tells us, would not have been sufficient to keep him from being exalted above measure, through the abundance of the revelations, unless there had been added some further cross, some "sting in the flesh," as he terms it, some secret affliction, of which we are not particularly informed, to humble him, and to keep him in a sense of his weak and dependent condition. St. Paul, pray for us.

THE ALTAR SANCTIFIETH

IF OUR SOUL were in perfect health, then riches and authority and strong powers of mind would be very suitable to us: but we are weak and diseased, and require so great a grace of God to bear these advantages well, that we may be well content to be without them.

Draw the following rule: use advantages, as far as given, with gratitude for what is really good in them, and with a desire to promote God's glory by means of them; but do not go out of the way to seek them. They will not on the whole make you happier, and they may make you less religious.

They must be instruments in our hands to promote the cause of God's truth. Their value and their happiness are imparted by the end to which they are dedicated. It is "the altar that sanctifieth the gift": but, compared with the end to which they must be directed, their real and intrinsic excellence is little indeed. "Glory be to the Father, etc."

FOR IMMORTALITY

THE TIME is short; year follows year, and the world is passing away. It is of small consequence to those who are beloved of God, and walk in the Spirit of truth, whether they pay or receive honor, which is but transitory and profitless. To the true Christian the world assumes another and more interesting appearance; it is no longer a stage for the great and noble, for the ambitious to fret in, and the wealthy to revel in; but it is a scene of probation. Every soul is a candidate for immortality. And the more we realize this view of things, the more will the accidental distinctions of nature or fortune die away from our view, and we shall be led habitually to pray, that upon every Christian may descend, in rich abundance, that heavenly grace which alone can turn this world to good account for us, and make it the path of peace and of life everlasting.

[93]

THY MARVELS have not been less since Thou didst ascend on high: Thy works of higher grace and more abiding fruit, wrought in the souls of men, the captives of Thy power, the ransomed heirs of Thy kingdom, led on from strength to strength till they appeared before Thy face in Sion. We crowd these all up into All Saints' day; the choicest deeds, the holiest lives, the noblest labors, the most precious sufferings, which the sun ever saw. Ye, holy Martyrs and Confessors, Rulers and Doctors of the Church, devoted priests and religious brethren; ye, poor of the earth and all toilers, princes and judges of the earth, young men and maidens, old men and children, the first fruits of all ranks, ages and callings, gathered each in your own time into the paradise of God, pray for us.

May the great multitude, which no man could number, the goodly fellowship of the Prophets, the noble army of Martyrs, the Children of the Holy Church Universal, who have rested from their labors, pray for us. Amen.

MUCH MORE VALUE

I OUGHT to praise and bless God that I have the gift of life. Thou hast pledged to us the ordinary means of sustenance which we naturally need: bread shall be given us; our water shall be sure; all these things shall be added unto us.

Thou hast not promised us what the world calls its great prizes. But still Thou hast promised that this shall be Thy rule, that thus shall it be fulfilled to us as Thy ordinary providence, viz., that life shall not be a burden to us, but a blessing, and shall contain more to comfort than to afflict. And giving us as much as this, Thou dost bid us to be satisfied with it; Thou dost bid us confess that we "have all" when we have so much: that we "abound" when we have enough; Thou dost promise us food, raiment and lodging; and Thou dost bid us, having food, and wherewith to be covered, with these to be content. For every creature of God is good, and nothing is to be rejected that is received with thanksgiving.

Thou dost not bid us to renounce the creation, but dost associate us with the most beautiful portions of it. Thou dost liken us to the flowers with which Thou hast ornamented the earth, and to the birds that live solitary under heaven, and make them the type of a Christian. Thou dost deny us Solomon's regal magnificence to unite us to the lilies of the field and the fowls of the air. "Be not solicitous for your life, what you shall eat. Behold the birds of the air. . . . Your heavenly Father feedeth them. Are you not of much more value than they? . . . Consider the lilies of the field . . . not even Solomon in all his glory was arrayed as one of these."

ACCEPTABLE SACRIFICE

HERE, then surely, is a matter for joy and thankfulness at all seasons, and not the least at times when, with a penitential forbearance, and according to the will of the Giver, not from thanklessness but from penance, we, for a while, more or less withhold from ourselves His good gifts. In times of self-denial, when we think it right to suspend our use of the good things of life, His gift, and to prove how salutary is the using them by the pain of abstaining from them,—especially in the weeks of Lent, when we are called on to try ourselves, as far as may be, by fasting or abstinence, or extra prayers or devotions that we may be brought closer to God,—let us thank God that He gives us the fruits of the earth in their seasons; that He gives us "bread out of the earth: and that wine may cheer the heart of man." Thus was it with our fathers of old time; thus is it with us now. Thus it was with St. Paul when he thanked the Philippians for "the gifts ye have sent me, the sweet savour of an acceptable sacrifice, well-pleasing to God."

AS SHEEP

SHEEP are defenceless, wolves are strong, and fierce. How prompt, how frightful, how resistless, how decisive, would be the attack of a troop of wolves on a few straggling sheep which fell in with them! And how lively, then, is the image which Our Lord uses to express the treatment which His followers were to receive from the world!

He Himself was the great Exemplar of

all such sufferings. When He was in the hands of His enemies, surrounded by a mad multitude, gazed on by relentless enemies, jeered at, struck, hurried along, tormented by rude soldiers, and at length, nailed to the cross, what was He emphatically but a sheep among wolves? "He shall be led as a sheep to the slaughter, and shall be dumb as a sheep before His shearer and He shall not open His mouth." And what He foretold of His followers, that the Psalmist had declared of them at an earlier time, and His Apostle applies it to them on its fulfillment. "As it is written," says St. Paul, "for Thy sake we are put to death all the day long. We are accounted as sheep for the slaughter." "Ye, holy martyrs, pray for us."

GOOD SHEPHERD

WHERE our Lord dwelt in the days of His flesh, the good shepherd gave his life for the sheep. "But the hireling fled." So too, on His Resurrection, while Mary wept, He did call her by her name, and she turned herself and knew Him by the ear Whom she had not known by the eye. "He calleth His own sheep by name."

Again, the office of a shepherd was lowly and simple. Yet no such title of earth could the Good Shepherd give to Himself, ever so lowly or mean, which would fitly show us His condescension. His act and deed is too great even for His own lips to utter it. But He delights in the image contained in the Good Shepherd, as conveying to us some notion of the degradation, hardship, and pain which He underwent for our sake. The Lord is my Shepherd. Lead me forth. Hear me, O Thou Shepherd of Israel. Gently lead me. Amen.

Christ, the Lord of angels, condescends to lay the lost sheep on His shoulders. By carrying it on His bosom is meant the love He bears the sheep, and the fullness of His grace; by carrying the sheep on His shoulders is signified the securing of the dwelling place. "Between His shoulders shall be rest." And if such were the figures, how much more was the Truth Itself, the good Shepherd, when He came, both guileless and heroic? He Who was "the carpenter's Son," Who was "meek and humble of heart," Who "went about doing good," Who "when He was reviled, reviled not again," and Who was "despised and most abject of men"? Have mercy on us, Thou "Man of Sorrows," Who didst "lay down Thy life for Thy sheep."

The planting of Thy Cross in my heart is sharp and trying; but the stately tree rears itself aloft and has fair branches and rich fruit and is good to look upon.

Let us "lift up our hearts," let us "lift them up unto the Lord!" Amen.

No earthly images can come up to the awful and gracious truth that God became the Son of Man—that the Word became flesh, and was born of woman. This ineffable mystery surpasses human words. No titles of earth can Christ give to Himself, ever so lowly or mean, which will fitly show us His condescension. His act and deed is too great even for His own lips to utter it. Yet He delights in the image of the Good Shepherd, as conveying to us, in such degree as we can receive it, some notion of the degradation, hardship and pain, which He underwent for our sake.

II

THE TRUTH

Setting the pattern of the Son of God ever before us, and studying so to act as if He were sensibly present, by look, voice, and gesture, to approve or blame us in all our private thoughts and all our intercourse with the world!

CHRIST THE KING

THE EPIPHANY is a season especially set apart for adoring the glory of Christ. The word may be taken to mean the manifestation of His glory, and leads us to the contemplation of Him as King upon His throne in the midst of His court, with His servants around Him, and His guards in attendance. At Christmas we commemorate His grace; and in Lent His temptation; and on Good Friday His sufferings and death; and on Easter Day His victory; and on Ascension His return to the Father; and in Advent we anticipate His second coming. And in all of these seasons He does something, or suffers something; but in the Epiphany and the weeks after it, we celebrate Him, not as on His field of battle, or in His solitary retreat, but as an august and glorious King; we view Him as the Object of our worship. Then only, during His whole earthly history, did He fulfil the type of Solomon, and held (as we may say) a court, and received the homage of His subjects, viz., when He

was an infant. His throne was His unde-
filed Mother's arms; His chamber of state
was a cottage or a cave; the worshippers
were the wise men of the East, and they
brought presents, gold, frankincense, and
myrrh. All around and about Him seemed
of earth, except to the eye of faith; one
note alone had He of divinity. As great
men of this world are often plainly
dressed, and look like other men, all but
as having some one costly ornament on
their breast or on their brow; so the Son of
Mary in His lowly dwelling, and in an
infant's form, was declared to be the Son
of God Most High, the Father of Ages,
and the Prince of Peace, by His star; a
wonderful appearance which had guided
the wise men all the way from the East,
even unto Bethlehem.

BEFORE HIM

THIS being the character of this Sacred
Season, our prayers throughout it, as far
as they are proper to it, are full of the
image of a king in his royal court, of a
sovereign surrounded by subjects, of a glorious prince upon a throne. There is no

thought of war, or of strife, or of suffering,
or of triumph, or of vengeance connected
with the Epiphany, but of august majesty,
of power, of prosperity, of splendour, of
serenity, of benignity. Now, if at any time,
it is fit to say, "The Lord is in His holy
temple; let all the earth keep silence before Him." Amen.

BENEFACTOR

"THE LIGHT shineth in darkness, and
the darkness does not comprehend It."
Thou didst seem like other men to the
multitude. Though conceived of the Holy
Ghost, Thou wast born of a poor mother,
who, when guests were numerous, was
thrust aside, and gave birth to Thee in a
place for cattle. O wondrous mystery, early
manifested, that even in birth Thou didst
refuse the world's welcome!

THY CLAIMS

THOU GREWEST up as the carpenter's
son, without education, so that when
Thou beganest to teach, Thy neighbors
wondered how one who had not learned

letters, and was bred to a humble craft, should become a prophet. Thou wast known as the kinsman and intimate of humble persons; so that the world pointed to them when Thou didst declare Thyself, as if their insufficiency was the refutation of Thy claims.

TO IMPART

THOU wast brought up in a town of low repute, so that even the better sort doubted whether good could come out of it. No; Thou wouldst not be indebted to this world for comfort, aid, or credit: for the world was made by Thee and the world knew Thee not. Thou camest to it as a benefactor, not as a guest; not to borrow from it, but to impart to it.

NO HOME

AND WHEN Thou didst grow up and begin to preach the kingdom of heaven, Thou, holy Jesus, didst take no more from the world then than before. Thou chosest the portion of those Saints who preceded and prefigured Thee, Abraham, Moses,

David, Elias, and Thy forerunner John
the Baptist. Thou didst live at large, without the ties of home or peaceful dwelling;
Thou didst live as a pilgrim in the land of
promise; Thou didst live in the wilderness.

Abraham had lived in tents in the country which his descendants were to enjoy.
David had wandered for seven years up
and down the same during Saul's persecutions. Moses had been a prisoner in the
howling wilderness all the way from
Mount Sinai to the borders of Canaan.
Elias wandered back again from Carmel to
Sinai. And the Baptist had remained in
the deserts from his youth.

Such in like manner was Thy manner
of life during Thy ministry; Thou wast
now in Galilee, now in Judea; Thou wast
found in the mountain, in the wilderness,
in the city; but Thou didst vouchsafe to
take no home, not even Thy Almighty
Father's temple at Jerusalem.

AUSTERITY

NOW ALL this seems quite independent
of the special objects of mercy which did
bring Thee upon earth. Though Thou
hadst still submitted Thyself by an incomprehensible condescension to the
death of the Cross at length, yet why didst
Thou from the first so spurn this world,
when Thou wast to die for its sins?

Thou mightest at least have had the
blessedness of brethren who believed in
Thee; Thou mightest have been happy
and revered at home; Thou mightest have
had honor in Thy own country; Thou
mightest have submitted but at last to
what Thou chosest from the first; Thou
mightest have delayed Thy voluntary sufferings till that hour when Thy Father's
and Thy own will made Thee the sacrifice
for sin.

THY PRESENCE

BUT THOU didst otherwise; and thus
Thou becamest a lesson to me who am
Thy disciple. Thou, who wast so separate
from the world, so present with the Father

even in the days of Thy flesh, callest upon me, Thy brother, as I am in Thee, to show that I am really what I have been made, by renouncing the world while in the world, and living as in the presence of Thee.

MY GLORY

LET ME consider that the perfection of my nature consists in the subjection and sacrifice of what is inferior in me to what is more excellent. Thou, Lord Jesus, who are the beginning and pattern of the new creature, didst live out of the body Thou wast in. Thy death indeed was required as an expiation; but why was Thy life so mortified, if such austerity be not man's glory? May a life of penance be my glory. Amen.

FACE TO FACE

YEAR after year, as it passes, brings us the same warnings again and again, and none perhaps more impressive than those with which it comes to us during Advent and Lent. The very frost and cold, rain and gloom, which now befall us, forebode the last dreary days of the world, and in religious hearts raise the thought of them.

When men in this world have to undergo any great thing, they prepare themselves beforehand, by thinking often of it, and they call this making up their mind. Any unusual trial they thus make familiar to them.

The day will be when I shall see Thee surrounded by Thy Angels. I shall be brought into that blessed company, in which all will be pure, all bright. Now I see in a mirror, obscurely; but then I shall see Thee face to face. Now I know in part; then, as St. Paul reminds me, shall I know fully, even as I have been fully known. Amen.

HIS REWARD

WHEN I rise, when I lie down; when I speak, when I am silent; when I act, and when I rest: whether I eat or drink, or whatever I do, may I never forget that "for all these God will bring thee into judgment." For He "cometh quickly," and His "reward is with Him, to render to every man according to his works." Amen.

POWERFUL NAME

WE ARE told that the devil, our adversary, as "a roaring lion goeth about, seeking whom he may devour"; and therefore are warned to "be sober and watch." And assuredly our true comfort lies, not in disguising the truth from ourselves, but in knowing something more than this;—that though Satan is against us, God is for us; that greater is He that is in us, than he that is in the world; and that He in every temptation will make a way for us to escape, that we may be able to bear it.

Now my great security against sin lies in being shocked at it. Eve gazed and reflected when she should have fled.

God does His part most surely; and Satan too does his part: I alone am unconcerned. Heaven and hell are at war for me, yet I trifle, and let life go on at random. Heaven and hell are before me as my own future abode, one or other of them; let my own interest move me as well as God's mercy. Directly I am made aware of the temptation, I shall, if I am wise, turn my back upon it, without waiting to think and reason about it; I shall engage my mind in other thoughts. There are temptations when this advice is especially necessary; but under all it is highly seasonable.

SAVIOUR

AT FIRST my conscience tells me, in a plain straightforward way, what is right and what is wrong; but when I trifle with this warning, my reason becomes perverted, and comes in aid of my wishes, and deceives me to my ruin. Then I begin to find that there are arguments available in behalf of bad deeds, and I listen to these till I come to think them true; and then, if perchance better thoughts return, and I make some feeble effort to get at the truth really and sincerely, I find my mind by that time so bewildered that I scarcely know right from wrong.

When, then, Satan comes against me, let me recollect I am already dedicated, made over, to God; I am God's property, I have no part with Satan and his works, I am servant to another, I am espoused to Christ. When Satan comes against me, let me fear not, waver not! but pray to God, and He will help me. Let me say to Satan with David, "Thou comest to me with a sword; but I come to thee in the name of the Lord of hosts." Thou comest to me with temptation; thou wouldest kill me, nay, thou wouldest make me kill myself with sinful thoughts, words and deeds; thou wouldest make me a self-murderer, tempting me by evil companions, and light conversation, and pleasant sights, and strong stirrings of heart; thou wouldest make me profane the Lord's day by riot; thou wouldest keep me from Church; thou wouldest make my thoughts rove when they should not; thou wouldest tempt me to drink, and to curse, and to swear, and to jest, and to lie, and to steal; but I know thee; thou art Satan, and I come unto thee in the name of the Living God, of Jesus Christ my Saviour.

That is a powerful name, which can put to flight all foes: Jesus is a name at which devils tremble. To speak it, is to scare away all bad thoughts. I come against thee in His All-powerful, All-conquering Name. David came on with a staff; my staff is the Cross—the Holy Cross on which Christ suffered, in which I glory; which is my salvation. David chose five smooth stones out of the brook, and with them he smote the giant. I, too, have armour, not of this world, but of God; a weapon which the world despises, but which is powerful in God—Jesus! Amen.

REPENTANCE

"O TASTE, and see that the Lord is sweet: blessed is the man that hopeth in Him." We see by these words what love Almighty God has towards us, and what claims He has upon our love. He is the Most High, and All-Holy. He inhabiteth eternity; we are but worms compared with Him. He would not be less happy though He had never created us; He would not be less happy though we were all blotted out again from creation.

But He is the God of love; He brought us all into existence, because He found satisfaction in surrounding Himself with happy creatures: He made us innocent, holy, upright, and happy. And when Adam fell into sin and his descendants after him, then ever since He has been imploring us to return to Him, the Source of all good, by true repentance. "Turn ye, turn ye," He says, "why will ye die? As I live I desire not the death of the wicked." "What is there that I ought to do more to my vineyard that I have not done to it?" May I be a different being from what I was before.

Before, I took things as they came, and thought no more of one thing than of another. But now every event has a meaning; it is God's, not my own estimate of whatever occurs; I recollect times and seasons; and the world, instead of being like the stream which the countryman gazed on, ever in motion and never in progress, is a various and complicated drama, with parts and with an object; God's providence. May I ever be His fruitful vineyard. Amen.

DWELL ON THEM

ONLY THINK of Him, when in His wounded state, and without garment on, He had to creep up the ladder, as He could, which led Him up to the Cross high enough for His murderers to nail Him to it; and consider *who* it was that was in that misery.

Or again, view Him dying, hour after hour bleeding to death; and how? in peace? no; with His arms stretched out, and His face exposed to view, and any one who pleased coming and staring at Him, mocking Him, and watching the gradual ebbing of His strength, and the approach of death.

These are some of the appalling details which the Gospels contain, and surely they were not recorded for nothing; but that we might dwell on them. "Was crucified, died and was buried."

WITH HER

IF THESE were the feelings of the people, what were St. John's feelings, or St. Mary Magdalene's, or our Blessed Mother's? Do we desire to be of this company? do we desire, according to His own promise, to be rather blessed than the womb that bore Him, and the paps that He sucked? do we desire to be as His brother, and sister, and mother? Then, surely, ought we to have some portion of that mother's sorrow! When He was on the Cross and she stood by, then, according to Simeon's prophecy, a sword pierced through her soul. What is the use of our keeping the memory of His cross and passion, unless we lament and are in sorrow with her? Mother of sorrows, pray for us.

PENITENT THIEF

WE, EVERY one of us, shall one day rise from our graves, and see Jesus Christ; we shall see Him who hung on the Cross, we shall see His wounds, we shall see the marks in His hands, and in His feet, and in His side. Do we wish to be of those, then, who wail and lament or of those who rejoice? If we would not lament at the sight of Him then, we must lament at the thought of Him now.

Let us prepare to meet our God; let us come into His presence whenever we can; let us try to fancy as if we saw the Cross and Him upon it; let us draw near to it; let us beg Him to look on us as He did on the penitent thief, and let us say to Him, "Lord remember me when Thou shalt come into Thy kingdom."

CONFORMED

NONE knows so well how vain is the world's praise, as he who has it. And why is this? It is, in a word, because the soul was made for religious employments and pleasures; and hence, that no temporal blessings, however exalted or refined can satisfy it. As well might we attempt to sustain the body on chaff, as to feed and nourish the immortal soul with the pleasures and occupations of the world.

Let me then rouse myself and turn from man to God; what have I to do with the world, who from my infancy have been put on my journey heavenward? Take up my cross and follow Christ. He went through shame far greater than can be mine. Do I think He felt nothing when He was lifted up on the Cross to public gaze, amid the contempt and barbarous triumphings of His enemies, the Pharisees, Pilate and His Roman guard, Herod and his men of war, and the vast multitude collected from all parts of the world? They all looked on Him with hatred and insult; yet He endured, "despising the shame." It is a high privilege to be allowed to be conformed to Christ. "We adore Thee, O Christ, and bless Thee. Because by Thy holy cross, Thou hast redeemed the world."

MY CROSS

CHRIST bids me take up my cross; therefore I accept the daily opportunities which occur of yielding to others, when I need not yield, and of doing unpleasant services, which I might avoid. He bids those who would be highest, live as the lowest: therefore, let me turn from ambitious thoughts, and (as far as I religiously may) make resolve against taking on authority and rule. He bids me sell and give alms; therefore, let me hate to spend money on myself. Shut my ears to praise, when it grows loud: set my face like a flint, when the world ridicules, and smile at its threats. Learn to master my heart, when it would burst forth into vehemence, or prolong a barren sorrow, or dissolve into unseasonable tenderness. Curb my tongue, and turn away my eye, lest I fall into temptation. Avoid the dangerous air which relaxes me, and brace myself upon the heights. Be up at prayer a great while before day, and seek the true, my only Bridegroom.

So shall self-denial become natural to me, and a change come over me, gently and imperceptibly; and, like Jacob, I shall lie down in the waste, and shall soon see Angels, and a way opened for me into heaven. Amen.

SELF-DENIAL

OUR LORD says, "If any man will come after Me, let him deny himself, and take up his cross daily, and follow me." Here He shows us from His own example what Christian self-denial is. It is taking on us a cross after His pattern, not a mere re-fraining from sin, for He had no sin, but a giving up what we might lawfully use. This was the peculiar character in which Christ came on earth. It was this spontaneous and exuberant self-denial which brought Him down.

He who was one with God, took upon Him our nature, and suffered death. And why? To save us whom He needed not to save. Thus He denied Himself, and took up His cross. This is the very aspect in which God, as revealed in Scripture, is distinguished from that exhibition of His glory, which nature gives us: power, wisdom, love, mercy, long-suffering. These attributes, though far more fully and clearly displayed in Scripture than in nature, still are in their degree seen on the face of the visible creation; but self-denial, if it may be said, this incomprehensible attribute of Divine Providence, is disclosed to us only in Scripture. "God so loved the world, as to give His only begotten Son."

Here is self-denial. And the Son of God so loved us, that being rich He became poor for our sakes. Here is our Saviour's self-denial. He pleased not Himself. "Jesus meek and humble of Heart, make our hearts like unto Thine."

HIS EXAMPLE

HE ROSE above the atmosphere of sin, sorrow and remorse, which broods over it. He entered into the region of peace and joy, into the pure light, the dwelling-place of Angels, the courts of the Most High, through which resound continually the chants of blessed spirits and the praises of the Seraphim. There He entered, leaving His brethren in due season to come after Him, by the light of His example, and the grace of His Spirit.

OPENED

YET, though forty days was a long season for Him to stay, it was but a short while for the Apostles to have Him among them. What feeling must have been theirs, when He parted from them? So late found, so early lost again. Hardly recognized, and then snatched away. The history of the two disciples at Emmaus was a figure or picture of the condition of the eleven. Their eyes were holden that they should not know him, while He talked with them for three years; then suddenly they were opened, and He forthwith vanished away.

LIVING BREAD

SO HAD it been, I say, with all of them. "Have I been so long a time with you, and have you not known Me?" had already been His expostulation with one of them.

They had not known Him all through His ministry. Peter, indeed, had confessed Him to be the Christ, the Son of the Living God; but even he showed inconsistency and change of mind in his comprehension of this great truth. But after His resurrection it was otherwise: Thomas touched His hands and His side, and said, "My Lord and my God"; in like manner, they all began to know Him; at length they recognized Him as the Living Bread which came down from heaven, and was the Life of the world. "Give us this day our daily bread, etc."

HID WITH CHRIST

IT IS then the duty and the privilege of all disciples of our glorified Saviour, to be exalted and transfigured with Him; to live in heaven in their thoughts, motives, aims, desires, likings, prayers, praises, intercession, even while they are in the flesh; to look like other men, to be busy like other men, to be passed over in the crowd of men, or even to be scorned or oppressed, as other men may be, but the while to have a secret channel of communication with the Most High, a gift the world knows not of; to have their life hid with Christ in God. Amen.

SHADOWS FLEE AWAY

ON THIS DAY God has done His greatest work. Let us think of it and of Him. Let us rejoice in the Day which He has made, and let us be willing in the Day of His Power. This is Easter Day. Let us say this again and again to ourselves with fear and great joy. As children say to themselves, "This is the spring," or "This is the sea," trying to grasp the thought, and not let it go; as travellers in a foreign land say, "This is that great city," or "This is that famous building," knowing it has a long history through centuries, and vexed with themselves that they know so little about it; so let us say, This is the Day of Days, the Royal Day, the Lord's Day.

This is the Day on which Christ arose from the dead; the Day which brought us salvation. It is a Day which has made us greater than we know. It is our Day of rest, the true Sabbath. Christ entered into His rest, and so do we. It brings us, in figure, through the grave and gate of death to our season of refreshment in Abraham's bosom. We have had enough of weariness, and dreariness, and listlessness, and sorrow, and remorse. We have had enough of this troublesome world. We have had enough of its noise and din. Noise is its best music. But now there is stillness; and it is a stillness that speaks.

We know how strange the feeling is of perfect silence after continued sound. Such is our blessedness now. Calm and serene days have begun; and Christ is heard in them, and His still small voice, because the world speaks not. Let us only put off the world, and we put on Christ. The receding from one is an approach to the other. We have now for some weeks been trying, through His grace, to unclothe ourselves of earthly wants and desires. May that unclothing be unto us a clothing upon of things invisible and imperishable! May we grow in grace, and in the knowledge of Our Lord and Saviour, season after season, year after year, till He takes to Himself, first one, then another, in the order He thinks fit, to be separated from each other for a little while, to be united together forever, in the kingdom of His Father and our Father, His God and our God.

Let us, as far as is permitted us, approach Him, who walked upon the sea, and rebuked the wind, and multiplied the loaves, and turned the water into wine, and made the clay give sight, and entered through the closed doors, and came and vanished at His will. Let us see Him by faith though our eyes are holden, that we know it not. Evermore may He so be with us, a gracious Lord, whose garments smell of myrrh, aloes, and cassia, of spikenard and saffron, calamus and cinnamon, and all trees of frankincense, myrrh, and aloes, with all the chief spices. So He be with us evermore, moving our hearts within us, until the day break and the shadows flee away. Amen.

REPOSE IN ONE GOD

ALL GOD's providences, all God's dealings with us, all His judgments, mercies, warnings, deliverances, tend to peace and repose as their ultimate issue. All our troubles and pleasures here, all our anxieties, fears, doubts, difficulties, hopes, encouragements, afflictions, losses, attainments, tend this one way.

After Christmas, Easter, and Whitsuntide, comes Trinity Sunday, and the weeks that follow; and in like manner, after our soul's anxious travail; after the birth of the Spirit; after trial and temptation; after sorrow and pain; after daily dyings to the world; after daily risings unto holiness; at length comes that "rest which remaineth unto the people of God."

After the fever of life; after weariness and sicknesses; fightings and despondings; languor and fretfulness; fightings and failing, struggling and succeeding; after all the changes and chances of this troubled unhealthy state, at length comes death, at length the White Throne of God, at length the Beatific Vision.

After restlessness comes rest, peace, joy;—our eternal portion, if we be worthy;—the sight of the Blessed Three, the Holy One; the Three that bear witness in heaven; in light unapproachable; in glory without spot or blemish; without variableness, or shadow of turning.

The Father God, the Son God, the

Holy Ghost God; the Father Lord, the Son Lord and the Holy Ghost Lord; the Father uncreate, the Son uncreate, and the Holy Ghost uncreate; the Father incomprehensible, the Son incomprehensible, and the Holy Ghost incomprehensible.

For there is one Person of the Father, another of the Son, and another of the Holy Ghost; and such as the Father is, such is the Son, and such is the Holy Ghost; and yet there are not three Gods, nor three Lords, nor three incomprehensibles, nor three uncreated; but one God, one Lord, one uncreated, and one incomprehensible.

Let us look forward to the time when this world will have passed away and all its delusions; and when we, when every one born of woman, must either be in heaven or in hell. Let us desire to hide ourselves under the shadow of His wings. Let us beg Him to give us an understanding heart, and that love of Him which is the instinct of the new creature, and the breath of spiritual life.

Let us pray Him to give us the spirit of obedience, of true dutifulness; an honest spirit, earnestly set to do His will, with no secret ends, no self designs of our own, no preferences of the creature to the Creator, but open, clear, conscientious, and loyal. So will He vouchsafe as time goes on, to take up His abode in us; the Spirit of Truth, whom the world cannot receive, will dwell in us, and be in us, and Christ "will love us, and will manifest Himself to us," and "the Father will love us, and They will come unto us, and make Their abode with us."

And when at length the inevitable hour comes, we shall be able meekly to surrender our souls, our sinful yet redeemed souls, in much weakness and trembling, with much self-reproach and deep confession, yet in firm faith, and in cheerful hope, and in calm love, to God the Father, God the Son, God the Holy Ghost, the Blessed Three, the Holy One; Three Persons, One God; our Creator, our Redeemer, our Sanctifier, our Judge. Amen.

When Christ called St. Paul, he "was not disobedient to the heavenly vision." Let us desire to know His voice; let us pray for the gift of watchful ears and a willing heart. He does not call all men in one way; He calls us each in His own way.

HEREAFTER

JOY, if it be Christian joy, the refined joy of the mortified and persecuted, makes men peaceful, serene, thankful, gentle, affectionate, sweet-tempered, pleasant, hopeful; it is graceful, tender, touching, winning. All this were the Christians of the New Testament, for they had obtained what they desired. They had desired to sacrifice the kingdom of the world and all its pomps for the love of Christ, whom they had seen, whom they loved, in whom they believed, in whom they delighted; and when their wish was granted, they could but be glad in that day and rejoice; for behold, their reward was great in heaven: blessed were they, thrice blessed, because they in their lifetime had evil things, and their consolation was to come hereafter.

Such was the joy of the first disciples of Christ, to whom it was granted to suffer shame and to undergo toil for His Name's sake; and such holy, gentle graces were the fruit of this joy, as every part of the Gospels and Epistles shows us. "We glory also in tribulations," says St. Paul.

PEACE

IF HE is in the midst of us, how shall we be moved? If Christ has died and risen again, what death can come upon us, though we be made to die daily? What sorrow, pain, humiliation, trial, but must end as His has ended, in a continual resurrection into His new world, and in a nearer and nearer approach to Him? He pronounced a blessing over His Apostles, and they have scattered it far and wide all over the earth unto this day. It runs as follows: "Peace I leave with you, My peace I give unto you; not as the world giveth do I give unto you." "These things I have spoken to you, that in Me you may have peace. In the world you shall have distress; but have confidence. I have overcome the world."

BLESS ME

WHERE TWO or three are gathered together in Christ's Name, He is in the midst of them. Believe that, were your eyes opened, as the young man's were, you would see horses and chariots of fire round about. God's arm is not shortened, though man does not believe. He does His wonders in spite of us. Elias went to heaven by miracle, and one man only saw it; but a miracle was done nevertheless. Angels are among us, and are powerful to do anything. And they do wonders for the believing, which the world knows nothing about.

According to our faith, so it is done unto us. Only believe, and all things are ours. We shall have clear and deeply-seated realization in our minds of the reality of the invisible world, though we cannot communicate them to others, or explain them. Like Jacob may I wrestle with the angel till morning and though it be the break of day, I will not let him go. "I will not let thee go, except thou bless me." May the holy angel of the Lord be with me in my journey, and bring me through safe. Amen.

THAT LITTLE

START now, with this holy season, and rise with Christ. See, He offers you His hand; He is rising; rise with Him. Mount up from the grave of the old Adam; from

grovelling cares, and jealousies, and fretfulness, and worldly aims; from the thral-
dom of habit, from the tumult of passion,
from the fascinations of the flesh, from a
cold, wordly, calculating spirit, from fri-
volity, from selfishness, from effeminacy,
from self-conceit and highmindedness.
Henceforth set about doing what it is so
difficult to do, but what should not, must
not be left undone; watch, and pray, and
meditate, that is, according to the leisure
which God has given you. Give freely of
your time to your Lord and Saviour, if you
have it. If you have little, show your sense
of the privilege by giving that little.

HID IN HIM

SHOW that your heart and your desires,
show that your life is with your God. Set
aside every day times for seeking Him.
Humble yourself that you have been hitherto so languid and uncertain. Live more
strictly to Him; take His yoke upon your
shoulder; live by rule. I am not calling on
you to go out of world, or to abandon
your duties in the world, but to redeem
the time; not to give hours to mere amuse-

ment or society, while you give minutes to Christ; not to pray to Him only when you are tired, and fit for nothing but sleep; not altogether to omit to praise Him, or to intercede for the world and the Church; but in good measure to realize honestly the words "set your affection on things above"; and to prove that you are His, in that your heart is risen with Him, and your life hid in Him. Amen.

BENEDICITE

WHEN God gives us grace to repent, when He enables us to chasten heart and body, to Him be praise; and for that very reason, while we do so, we must not cease rejoicing in Him. We must rejoice, while we afflict ourselves.

Though we must be temperate and bring our body into subjection, lest we become castaways; yet through God alone we can do this; and while He is with us, we cannot but be joyful; for His absence only is a cause for sorrow.

The Three Holy Children walked in the midst of the flames and called on all the works of God to rejoice with them;

on sun, moon, and stars of heaven, nights and days, showers and dew, frost and cold, lightnings and clouds, mountains and hills, green things upon the earth, seas and floods, fowls of the air, beasts and cattle, and children of men; praise and bless the Lord and magnify Him forever. Amen.

All ye works of the Lord, bless the Lord: praise and exalt Him above all forever. O ye Angels of the Lord, bless the Lord.

INFINITE

I HAVE no such trial as the Three Holy Children; I have no such awful suspense as theirs, I attempt for the most part what I know; I begin what I think I can go through. I can neither instance their faith nor equal their rejoicing; yet I can imitate them so far, as to look abroad into this fair world, which God made very good, while I mourn over the evil which Adam brought into it; to hold communion with what I see there, while I seek Him who is invisible; to admire it, while I abstain from it; to acknowledge God's love, while I deprecate His wrath; to confess that,

[135]

many as are my sins, His grace is greater. My sins are more in number than the hairs of my head; yet even the hairs of my head are all numbered by Thee.

Thou dost count my sins, and, as Thou dost count, so canst Thou forgive; for that reckoning, great though it be, comes to an end; but Thy mercies fail not, and Thy Son's merits are infinite. Amen.

O give thanks to the Lord, because He is good; because His mercy endureth for ever and ever. Amen.

HOLY SPIRIT

IT WAS promised that "There shall be no more waters of a flood to destroy all flesh"; and yet a flood there was to be, a mighty flood of waters, all-compassing, all absorbing, in God's good time, and in His merciful foreknowledge, when He spake the former word; but not to destroy all flesh, but to save it. And in its season, this second, and more wonderful and more gracious deluge came to pass; the rain of grace descended; the heavens dropped down dew from above, and the clouds rained the just; the rain fell, and the floods came, and the

winds blew; the sea made a noise, and all
that therein is; the round world, and they
that dwell therein; the earth began to fill
with the knowledge of the glory of the
Lord; for "the Spirit of the Lord hath
filled the whole world; and that which con-
taineth all things hath knowledge of the
voice."

COMFORTER

HOW DIFFERENT a fulfilment was this
from that for which the Apostles had been
waiting! For ten days had they waited for
the fulfilment of a promise, the coming of
a Comforter. And surely they imagined,
that such as Christ had been, would be
the Paraclete which was to come. Christ
was a present, visible, protector; a man,
with man's voice and man's figure. Who
was to be their Comforter, how could they
conjecture, seeing He was to be such, that
it was expedient for them that Christ
should depart?

For such an one they waited during ten
days to guide them into all truth, little
deeming that knowledge about Himself
was one main portion of the truth He had
to teach them; and then, when they were

waiting for this Angelic Messenger, Prophet, and Lawgiver, one higher than all created strength and wisdom, suddenly came down upon them.

Such was the coming of the Comforter; He who is infinitely personal, who is one and individual above all created beings, who is the One God, absolutely, fully, perfectly, simply, He it was who vouchsafed to descend upon the Apostles.

He came to teach them fully, what our Lord had but in part revealed; and hence too it followed that the consolation which the Spirit vouchsafed differed from that which they had received from Christ, just as the encouragements and rewards bestowed upon children, are far other than those which soothe and stimulate grown men in arduous duties.

MY SPIRIT

SUCH was the power of the Spirit in the beginning, when He vouchsafed to descend as an invisible wind, as an outpoured flood. Thus he changed the whole face of the world. For a while men went on as usual, and dreamed not what was coming;

and when they were roused from their fast sleep, the work was done; it was too late for aught else but impotent anger and an hopeless struggle. The kingdom was taken away from them and given to another people. The ark of God moved upon the face of the waters. It was borne aloft by the power, greater than human, which had over-spread the earth, and it triumphed, "with an army not by might but by my spirit saith the Lord of hosts."

FLOOD OF GRACE

AND WHAT the power of the Spirit has been in the world at large, that it is also in every human heart to which it comes. The characteristics of the Spirit's influence are that it is the same everywhere, that it is silent, that it is gradual, that it is thorough; not violent, or abrupt or fitful. Vehemence, tumult, confusion, are not attributes of that benignant flood with which God has replenished the earth. That flood of grace is sedate, majestic, gentle in its operation.

EVERY UNDERSTANDING

IT CLAIMS the whole man for God. Any spirit which is content with what is short of this, which does not lead us to utter self-surrender and devotion; which reserves something for ourselves; which indulges our self-will; which flatters this or that natural inclination or affection; which does not tend to consistency of religious character is not from God. The heavenly influence which He has given us is as intimately present, and as penetrating—as catholic—in an individual heart as it is in the world at large. It is everywhere, in every faculty, every affection, every design, every work, "destroying every height that exalteth itself against the knowledge of God, and bringing into captivity every understanding unto the obedience of Christ."

TO PRAY

LET US but raise the level of God's love in our hearts, and it will rise in the world. He who attempts to set up God's kingdom in his heart, furthers it in the world. He whose prayers come up for a memorial before God, opens the "flood gates of heaven, and the foundations of the great deep," and the waters rise. He who with Christ goes up into the mountain to pray, or with St. Peter seeks the house-top, or with Mary is in the company with many, praying, or with Paul and Silas, singing praises at midnight, he is overcoming the world, let the world do what it will.

THAT SPIRIT

LET these instances be my encouragement now. Let me try to serve God more strictly than heretofore; let me pray Him to send down that Spirit which converted the world in the beginning, and He surely will answer my prayers far beyond what I think or hope. Amen.

HIS MOTHER

JESUS had been with her for thirty years. She had borne Him, she had nursed Him, she had taught Him. And when He had reached twelve years old, at the age when the young may expect to be separated from their parents, He had only become more intimately one with them, for we are told that "He went down with them, and came to Nazareth, and was subject to them." Eighteen years had passed away since this occurred. St. Joseph had been taken to his rest. Mary remained; but from Mary, His Mother, He must now part, for the three years of His ministry.

He had gently intimated this to her at the very time of His becoming subject to her, intimated that His heavenly Father's work was a higher call than any earthly duty. "Did you not know," He said, when found in the Temple, "that I must be about My Father's business?" The time was now come when this was to be fulfilled, yet at His mother's request, He turned water into wine. "This beginning of miracles did Jesus in Cana of Galilee."

Virgin, all powerful, may every Church which is dedicated to thee, every altar which is raised under Thy invocation, every image which represents thee, every litany in thy praise, every Hail Mary for thy continual memory, but make me imitate the One Who for my sake "did not shrink from the Virgin's womb." Amen.

TEMPER THINGS

WE FEEL and understand that it is good to bear the yoke in our youth, good to be in trouble, good to be in low estate, good to be poor, good to be despised; if in imagination we put ourselves at the feet of those mortified men of old time, who, after St. Paul's pattern, died daily, and knew no one after the flesh; if we feel all this, and are conscious we feel it: let us not boast. Why? because of a surety such feelings are a pledge to us that God will in some way or other give them exercise. He gives them to us that He may use them. He gives us the opportunity of using them. Dare not to indulge in high thoughts; be cautious of them, and refrain; they are the shadows of coming trials; they are not given for nothing; they are given for an end; that end is coming.

Count the cost; never does God give faith but He tries it; never does He implant the wish to sit on His right hand and on His left, but He fulfils it by making us wash our brethren's feet. O fearful imaginations, which are sure to be realized! O dangerous wishes, which are heard and forthwith answered! Only may God temper things to us, that nothing may be beyond our strength!

DAVID'S HOPE

GOD is with us. We are told in Scripture to cast all our care upon Him, for He hath care of us; to ask and we shall receive; and surely what Jacob felt and said, will in its degree,—nay, rather more abundantly—be fulfilled in our case. "I am not worthy of the least of all Thy mercies, and of Thy truth which Thou hast fulfilled to Thy servant." "God, in whose sight my fathers Abraham and Isaac walked, God who feedeth from my youth until this day; the Angel that delivereth me from all evils."

Is it not, I may say, most touching and affecting to read in patriarchal history things which are fulfilled in us at this latter time?—but He is the Lord, He changes not. You may see what He is to us, by what Jacob tells us He was to him. Scripture gives certain specimens or criteria, what it is to have God with us, to be guided by God, as in the history of Jacob or of David. Now consider Jacob's life and confessions, or consider David's overflowings of heart in the Psalms—are they not in our measure ours also? Is there not a sympathy of heart, is there not a concordant testimony as to God's providences in the ancient Saints and in ourselves? Well, then, are we not therefore in their case? do not we stand with them? have not *we* the God of Jacob for our help, and is not David's Lord and David's hope ours also?

INFIRMITIES

THAT TROUBLE and sorrow are in some especial sense the lot of the Christian, is plain again from Scripture. For instance, St. Paul and St. Barnabas remind the disciples "that through many tribulations we must enter into the kingdom of God." Again, St. Paul says, "Yet so, if we suffer with Him, that we may also be glorified with Him." Again, "If we suffer, we shall also reign with Him." Again, "and all that will live godly in Christ Jesus, shall suffer persecution." Again, St. Peter, "But if doing well, you suffer patiently, this is thankworthy before God; for unto this are you called." And our Saviour declares, that those who have given up the relations of this world "for His sake and the Gospel's" shall receive "an hundred-fold" now, "with persecutions." And St. Paul speaks in his own case of his "perils," by sea and land, from friend and foe, without and within him, of the body and of the soul. Yet, he adds, "I wilt glory of the things which concern mine infirmities." Jacob and David, Peter, Paul and Barnabas, pray for us.

CONFESSORS AND MARTYRS

OUR LORD said of St. Bartholomew, "Behold an Israelite, in whom indeed there is no guile." Just before this apostle was called, he was engaged in meditation or prayer, in the privacy which a fig-tree's shade afforded him. Quietness without, guilelessness within. This was the tranquil preparation for great dangers and sufferings! If it should please God suddenly to bring me forward to great trials, as He did His Apostles, may I not be taken by surprise, but be found to have made a private or domestic life a preparation for the achievements of Confessors and Martyrs! Amen.

STS. JOHN AND JAMES

THE TWO holy brothers, those holy Apostles, said, "We are able," and in truth they were enabled to do and to suffer as they said. St. James was given strength to be steadfast unto death, the death of martyrdom, being slain with the sword in Jerusalem. St. John, his brother, had still more to bear, dying last of the Apostles, as St. James first. He had to bear bereavement, first, of his brother, then of the other Apostles. He had to bear a length of years in loneliness, exile and weakness.

He had to experience the dreariness of being solitary, when those whom he loved had been summoned away. He had to live in his own thoughts, without familiar friend, with those only about him who belonged to a younger generation. Of him were demanded by his gracious Lord, as pledges of his faith, all his eye loved and his heart held converse with. He was a man moving his goods into a far country, who at intervals and by portions sends them before him, till his present abode is well-nigh unfurnished. He sent forward his friends on their journey, while he stayed behind himself that there might be those in heaven to have thoughts of him, to look out for him and receive him when his Lord shall call.

He sent before him, also, other still more voluntary pledges and acts of faith— a self-denying walk, a zealous maintenance of the truth, fasting and prayers, labors of love, a virgin life, buffettings from the heathens, persecution and banishment. Well might so great a Saint say, at the end of his days, "Come, Lord Jesus!", as those who are weary of the night and wait for the morning.

All his thoughts, all his contemplations, desires and hopes were stored in the invisible world; and death, when it came, brought to him the sight of what he had worshipped, what he had loved, what he had held intercourse with, in years long passed away.

Then, when again brought into the presence of what he had lost, how would remembrance revive, and familiar thoughts long buried come to life! Who shall dare to describe the blessedness of those who find all their pledges safe returned to them, all their ventures abundantly and beyond measure satisfied? Saints John and James, pray for us.

ST. PAUL

THE OVERTHROW of the wisdom of the world was one of the earliest, as well as the noblest of the triumphs of the Church, after the pattern of her Divine Master who took His place among the doctors before He preached His new Kingdom, and opposed Himself to the world's power. St. Paul, the learned Pharisee, was the first fruits of that gifted company, in whom the pride of science is seen prostrated before the foolishness of preaching.

KNOWLEDGE

FROM his day to this the Cross has enlisted under its banner all those great endowments of mind, which in former times had been expended on vanities, or dissipated in doubt and speculation. Yet St. Paul speaks of willingly losing all things for the excellence of the knowledge of Christ Jesus, my Lord, that I may gain Christ; that I may know Him; the power of His resurrection." And St. Peter: "the knowledge of Him who hath called us by His own proper glory and virtue." Amen.

WHAT TO DO

IF THERE is one point of character more than another which belonged to St. Paul, and discovers itself in all he said and did, it was his power of sympathising with his brethren, nay, with all classes of men. He went through trials of every kind, and this was their issue, to let him into the feelings, and thereby to introduce him to the hearts, of high and low, Jew and Gentile. He knew how to persuade, for he knew where lay the perplexity; he knew how to console, for he knew the sorrow. His spirit within him was as some delicate instrument, which, as the weather changed about him, as the atmosphere was moist or dry, hot or cold, accurately marked all its variations, and guided him what to do.

SAVE ALL

AND WHAT he was in persuasion, such he was in consolation. He himself gives this reason for his trials, speaking of Almighty God's comforting him in all his tribulation, in order that he might be able to comfort them who were in any trouble, by the exhortation, wherewith he himself was exhorted by God. To the Jews, a Jew, that he might gain the Jews; to the weak he became weak, that he might gain the weak. "I became all things to all men that I might save all."

THE TEST

OUR SIN will be if we idolize the work of our hands; if we love it so well as not to bear to part with it. The test of our faith lies in our being able to fail without disappointment. St. Paul, pray for us.

THEIR CALLING

WHEN St. Paul heard the voice from heaven, he said at once, trembling and astonished, "Lord, what wilt Thou have me to do?" This same obedient temper of his is stated or implied in the two accounts which he himself gives of his miraculous conversion. In the 22nd chapter of the Acts and in the 26th, after telling King Agrippa what the Divine Speaker said to him, he adds what comes to the same thing, "Whereupon, O King Agrippa, *I was not incredulous* to the heavenly vision."

Such is the account given us in St. Paul's case of that first step in God's gracious dealings with him, which ended in his eternal salvation. "Whom He foreknew, He also predestinated";—"whom He predestinated, them He also called"— here was the first act which took place in time—"and whom He called, them He also justified; and whom He justified, them He also glorified." Such is the Divine series of mercies; and you see that it was prompt obedience on St. Paul's part which carried on the first act of Divine grace into the second, which knit together the first mercy to the second. St. Paul was called when Christ appeared to him in the way; he was sanctified when Ananias came to baptize him; and it was prompt obedience which led him from his call to his baptism.

"Lord, what wilt Thou have me to do?" The answer was, "Arise, and go into the city (Damascus) and there it shall be told thee what thou must do." And when he came to Damascus, Ananias was sent to him by the same Lord who had appeared to him; and he reminded St. Paul of this when he came to him. The Lord had appeared for his call; the Lord had appeared for his sanctification.

This, then, is the lesson taught us by St. Paul's conversion, promptly to obey the call. If we do obey it, to God be the glory, for He it is who works in us. If we do not obey, to ourselves be all the shame, for sin and unbelief work in us. Such being the state of the case, let us take care to act accordingly,—being exceedingly alarmed lest we should *not* obey God's voice when He calls us, yet not taking praise or credit to ourselves if we *do* obey it. This has been the temper of all saints from the beginning —working out their salvation with fear and trembling, yet ascribing the work to Him who wrought them to will and do of His good pleasure; obeying the call, and giving thanks to Him who calls, to Him who fulfils in them their calling. Such is

the pattern afforded us by St. Paul. May
he pray for us.

FEAR AND TREMBLING

ST. PAUL says expressly of himself and
the other Apostles, that they were "men
of like passions" with the poor ignorant
heathen to whom they preached. And does
not his history show this? Do you not recollect what he was before his conversion?
Did he not rage like a beast of prey against
the disciples of Christ? And how was he
converted? by the vision of our Lord? Yes,
in one sense, but not by it alone; hear
his own words, "Whereupon, O King
Agrippa, I was not disobedient to the heavenly vision." His obedience was necessary
for his conversion; he could not obey without grace; but he would have received
grace in vain, had he not obeyed. And,
afterwards, was he at once perfect? No; for
he says expressly, "not as though I had
already attained, or were already perfect";
and elsewhere he tells us that he had a
"sting of the flesh, the angel of Satan to
buffet him"; and he was obliged to "bruise
his body and bring it into subjection, lest,

after he had preached to others, he should be himself a castaway." St. Paul conquered, as any one of us must conquer by "striving," struggling, "to enter in at the strait gate"; he "wrought out his salvation with fear and trembling," as we must do. St. Paul, pray for us.

GOD OF ISRAEL

SO WAS it with Jacob, when with his staff he passed over the Jordan. He too kept feast before he set out upon his dreary way. He received a father's blessing, and then was sent afar; he left his mother, never to see her face or hear her voice again. He parted with all that his heart loved, and turned his face towards a strange land. He went with the doubt, whether he should have bread to eat, or raiment to put on. He "came into the east country" and served a hard master: "day and night was I parched with heat, and with frost, and sleep departed from his eyes." O little did he think, when father and mother had forsaken him, and at Bethel he lay down to sleep on the desolate ground, because the sun was set and even had come, that there was the house of God and the gate of heaven, that the Lord was in that place, and would thence go forward with him whithersoever he went, till He brought him back to that river, who was then crossing it forlorn and solitary! May we too, always trustingly invoke "the most mighty God of Israel." Amen.

HIS TEMPLE

WHETHER we eat or drink, or whatever we do, to His glory must we do all, and if to His glory, to our great joy; for His service is perfect freedom; and what are the very Angels in heaven but His ministers? Nothing is evil but separation from Him; while we are allowed to visit His temple, we cannot but "go into His gates with praise and into His courts with hymns." "Is any," then, "of you sad? Let him pray. Is he cheerful in mind? Let him sing."

St. Paul did not look on this life with bitterness, complain of it morosely, or refuse to enjoy it; he was not soured, but he felt that if he had troubles in this world, he had blessings also; and he did not reject these, but made much of them.

HIS PRESENCE

CHEERFULNESS is a great Christian duty. Whatever be our circumstances, within or without, though "combats without, fears within" yet the Apostle's words are express, "Rejoice in the Lord *always*." That sorrow, that solicitude, that fear, that repentance, is not Christian which has not its portion of Christian joy; for "God is greater than our hearts," and no evil, past or future, within or without, is equal to this saying, that Christ has died and reconciled the world unto Himself. I am ever in His Presence, be I cast down, or be I exalted; and "in His Presence is the fulness of joy." "Thou shalt fill me with joy with thy countenance."

HOSANNA

WE HAVE a remarkable and solemn instance of the duty of keeping festival and rejoicing even in the darkest day, in our Lord's own history. If there was a season in which gloom was allowable, it was on the days and hours before His passion: but He who came to bring joy on earth and not sorrow; who came eating and drinking, because He was the true Bread from heaven; who changed the water into wine at a marriage feast, and fed the hungry thousands in the wilderness; even in that awful time when His spirit fainted within Him, when, as He testified, His soul was sorrowful, and He "prayed, that if it might be the hour pass from Him," and more solemnly and secretly, "if it be possible, let this chalice pass from Me"; He, our great Exemplar, kept the feast—nay, anticipated it, as if though He Himself was to be the very Paschal Lamb, still He was not thereby excused from sharing in the typical rite.

With desire did He desire to eat that passover with His disciples before He suffered. And a few days before it, He took part in a public and (as it were) triumphant pageant, as though the bitterness of death already passed. He came to Bethany, where He had raised Lazarus; and there they made Him a supper; and Mary took the precious ointment and poured it on His head, and anointed His feet, and the house was filled with the fragrance. And next the people took branches of palm-trees, and went forth to meet Him, and strewed their garments in the way, and cried, "Hosanna, blessed is He that cometh in the name of the Lord, the King of Israel."

CHEERFULNESS

THE SAME rule is to be observed even in the instance of personal penitence, which is on no account to be separated from the duty of Christian cheerfulness. Penitents are as little at liberty to release themselves from Christian joy as from Christian love; love alone can make repentance available; and where there is love, there joy must be present also. The true penance is not to put away God's blessings, but to add to chastisements. As Adam did not lose the flowers of Eden on his fall, but thorns and thistles sprung up around them; and he still had bread, but was forced to eat it in the sweat of his face; and as the Israelites ate their Paschal lamb with bitter herbs; so in like manner we show our repentance, not in rejecting what God gives, but in adding what sin deserves.

ON GUARD

AGAIN, how many are there, who bear half the trial God puts on them, but not the whole of it; who go on well for a time, and then fall away! Saul bore on for seven days, and fainted not; on the eighth day his faith failed him. Oh may we persevere to the end! Many fall away. Let us watch and pray. Let us not get secure. Let us not think it enough to have got through one temptation well; through our whole life we are on trial. When one temptation is over, another comes; and, perhaps, our having got through one well, will be the occasion of our falling under in the next, if we be not on our guard; because it may make us secure and confident, as if we had already conquered, and were safe.

OBEDIENT

SAUL wished that an act of worship and prayer should precede his battle; he desired to have God's blessing upon him; and perversely, while he felt that blessing to be necessary, he did not feel that the only way of gaining it was seeking it *in the way* which God had appointed; that, whereas God had not made him his minister, he could not possibly offer the burnt offering acceptable. Thus he deceived himself; and thus many men deceive themselves now; not casting off grace altogether, but choosing their own way for themselves, as Saul did, and fancying they can be religious without being obedient.

IN THE SPIRIT

ONCE MORE, how many are there, who, in a narrow grudging cold-hearted way, go by the letter of God's commandments, while they neglect the spirit! Instead of considering what Christ wishes them to do, they take His words one by one, and will only accept them in their bare necessary meaning. They do not open their hearts generously to the voice of a living and Kind Lord and Master speaking to them, but they take it to mean as little as it can. They are wanting in love. Saul was told to wait seven days—he *did* wait seven days; and then he thought he might do what he chose. He, in effect, said to Samuel, "I have done just what you told me." Yes, he fulfilled directions literally and rigidly, but not in the spirit of love. Had he loved the Word of God, he would not have been so precise and exact in his reckoning, but would have waited still longer. And, in like manner, persons now-a-days, imitating him, too often obey carnally in the letter, and not the spirit.

WITH THE HEART

HOW will all excuses, which sinners now make to blind and deaden their consciences, fail them in the Last Day! Saul had his excuses for disobedience. He did not confess he was wrong, but he argued; but Samuel with a word reproved, and convicted, and silenced, and sentenced him. And so in the day of Judgment all our actions will be tried by fire. The All-knowing, All-holy Judge, our Saviour Jesus Christ, will sit on His throne, and with the breath of His mouth He will scatter away all idle excuses on which men now depend; and the secrets of men's hearts will be revealed. Then shall be seen who it is that serveth God, and who serveth Him not; who serve Him with the lips, who with the heart; who are hypocrites, and who are true.

WHO DO IT

GOD give me grace to be in the number of those whose faith and whose love is without hypocrisy or pretence; who obey out of a pure heart and a good conscience; who sincerely wish to know God's will, and who do it as far as they know it! Amen.

GOD'S PRESENCE

"I AM filled to overflowing" is St. Paul's confession concerning his temporal condition, even in the midst of his trials. Those trials brought with them spiritual benefits; but, even as regarded this world, he felt he had cause for joy and thankfulness, in spite of sorrow, pains, labors, and self-denials. He did not look on this life with bitterness, complain of it morosely or refuse to enjoy it; he was not soured, as the children of men often are, by his trials; but he felt that if he had troubles in this world, he had blessings also; and he did not reject these, but made much of them. "For every creature of God is good, and nothing to be rejected that is received with thanksgiving: for it is sanctified by the word of God and prayer."

Gloom is no Christian temper; that repentance is not real, which has not love in it; that self-chastisement is not acceptable, which is not sweetened by faith and cheerfulness. We must live in sunshine, even when we sorrow; we must live in God's presence, we must not shut ourselves up in our own hearts, even when we are reckoning up our past sins. Our Father, who art in heaven, etc.

GIVING THANKS

"GIVING thanks always for all things in the name of our Lord Jesus Christ to God the Father." A great Apostle! St. Paul how could it be otherwise, considering what thou hadst been and what thou wast, transformed from an enemy to a friend, from a blind Pharisee to an inspired preacher!

THY HAND

LET ME trust I am on the whole serving God. Let me look back on my past life and I shall find how critical were moments and acts, which at the time seemed the most indifferent: as for instance, the school I was sent to as a child, the occasion of my falling in with those persons who have most benefited me, the seeming accidents which determined my calling. Thy hand is ever over Thy own.

Thou dost lead me forward by a way I know not of. I believe what I cannot see now, what I shall see hereafter. Amen.

TO OVERFLOWING

HOW BLESSED I am to come, day after day, quietly and calmly, to receive my Lord and Saviour. How soothing will one day be the remembrance of Thy past gifts! I shall remember how I got up early in the morning and how all things, light or darkness, sun or air, cold or freshness, breathed of Thee—of Thee, the Lord of glory, who stoodest over me, and camest unto me and gavest Thyself to me, and pouredst forth spiritual milk and honey for my sustenance, though I saw Thee not. Surely "I have received everything, and more than enough; I am filled to overflowing. To our God and Father be the glory through the endless ages. Amen."

NO TERMS

I THEREFORE sacrifice to Thee this cherished wish, this weakness, this scheme, this opinion: make me what Thou wouldst have me; I bargain for nothing; I make no terms; I seek for no previous information whither Thou art taking me: I will be what Thou wilt make me, and all that Thou wilt make me.

I say not, I will follow Thee whithersoever Thou goest, for I am weak; but I will give myself to Thee to lead me anywhither. I will follow thee in the dark, only begging Thee to give me strength according to my day. Try me, O Lord, and seek the ground of my heart; prove me, and examine my thoughts; look well if there be any wickedness in me; search each dark recess with Thy own bright light, and lead me in the way everlasting.

PERFORM IT

I CAN BEG everything: an honest purpose, an unreserved, entire submission of myself to my Maker, Redeemer and Judge. Let me beg Thee to aid me in my endeavor, and, as Thou hast begun a good work in me, to perform it until the day of my Lord Jesus. Amen.

ST. MATTHIAS

The rest of the Apostles had been chosen (as it were) as children, they had been heirs of the kingdom, while under tutors and governors, and, though Apostles, had not understood their calling, had had ambitious thoughts or desires. But St. Matthias came into his inheritance at once. He took upon himself at once, at his election, the power and the penalty of the Apostolate. No dreams of earthly prosperity could flit about that throne, which was reared over the grave of one who had been tried and had fallen, and under the immediate shadow of the cross of Him whom he had betrayed. St. Matthias, pray for us.

BEFORE THE THRONE

AN INNUMERABLE company of Angels, and the Spirits of the just;—we dwell under their shadow; we are baptized into their fellowship; we are allotted their guardianship; we are remembered, as we know in their prayers. We dwell in the very presence and court of God Himself, and of his Eternal Son our Saviour, who died for us, and rose again, and now intercedes for us before the Throne.

FELLOW SERVANTS

ANGELS are inhabitants of the world invisible, and concerning them much more is told us than concerning the souls of the faithful departed, because the latter "rest from their labors"; but the angels are actively employed among us in the Church. They are said to be ministering spirits, sent to minister to them, who shall receive the inheritance of salvation. Though they are so great, so glorious, so pure, so wonderful, that the very sight of them, if we were allowed to see them, would strike us to the earth, as it did the prophet Daniel, holy and righteous as he was, yet they are our fellow servants and our fellow workers, and they carefully watch over and defend the humblest of us. Angel of God, my guardian dear, etc.

CONVERSATION

THE WORLD of spirits, though unseen, is present; present, not future, not distant. It is not above the sky, it is not beyond the grave; it is now and here; the kingdom of God is among us. It is a practical truth, which is to influence our conduct. "Our conversation is in heaven; our life is hid with Christ in God."

EYES OF FAITH

O LORD, show Thyself; manifest Thyself; Thou that sittest between the cherubim, show Thyself; stir up Thy strength and come and help us. The earth that we see does not satisfy us; it is but a beginning; it is a promise of something beyond it; even when it is gayest, with all its blossoms on, and shows most touchingly what lies hid in it, yet it is not enough. What we see is the outward shell of an eternal kingdom; and on that kingdom we fix the eyes of our faith.

YE ANGELS

BLESSED servants of God, who have never tasted of sin; who are among us, though unseen, ever serving God joyfully on earth as well as in heaven; who minister to the redeemed in Christ, the heirs of salvation. It was an Angel who gave to the pool of Bethesda its healing quality. The fires on Mount Sinai, the thunder and lightnings, were the work of Angels; and in the Apocalypse we read of the Angels restraining the four winds. The earthquake at the Resurrection was the work of the Lord. O ye Angels of the Lord, bless ye the Lord, praise Him, and magnify Him for ever. Amen.

MINISTERING

SURELY we are not told in Scripture about the Angels for nothing, but for practical purposes. We cannot conceive a use of such knowledge more practical than to make it connect the sight of this world with the thought of another. Nor one more consolatory; for surely it is a great comfort to reflect that, wherever we go, we have those about us, who are ministering to all the heirs of salvation. Though we see them not, may they enlarge our view of the next world. Amen.

HIDE THEIR FACES

WHEN WE survey Thee, Almighty God, surrounded by Thy Holy Angels, Thy thousand thousands of ministering Spirits, and ten thousand times ten thousand standing before Thee, the idea of Thy awful majesty rises before us more powerfully and impressively. We begin to see how little we are, how altogether mean and worthless in ourselves; and how high Thou art, and fearful. The very lowest of Thy Angels is indefinitely above us in this our present state; how high then must be the Lord of Angels! The very seraphim hide their faces before Thy glory, while they praise Thee; how shamefaced then should we sinners be, when we come into Thy presence!

BE READY

THY CHURCH has lasted for these many centuries; it will last still, through the promised help of God the Holy Ghost; and that same promise which is made to it first as a body, is assuredly made also to every one of us who seeks grace from God through it. The grace of our Lord and Saviour is pledged to every one of us without measure, to give us all necessary strength and holiness when we pray for it. Amen.

When I kneel before Thy priest and confess my sins, let me think to myself, thus shall I one day kneel before Thy very footstool, in this flesh and blood also, though divine. I come with the thought of that awful hour before me, I come to confess my sin to Thee now, that Thou mayest pardon it, and I say, "Holy, holy, holy, Lord God, be merciful now, in the hour of my death and in the day of judgment."

Thou who wilt be my Judge, prepare me to be judged. Thou, who art to glorify me, prepare me to be glorified, that Thou mayest not take me unawares; but that when the Archangel sounds, and I am called to meet the Bridegroom, I may be ready. Amen.

MISSIONARIES

DID our Saviour come on earth suddenly, as He will one day visit it, in whom would He see the features of the Christians whom He and His Apostles left behind? Surely in those who give up home and friends, wealth and ease, good name and liberty of will, for the kingdom of heaven? Where shall we find the image of St. Paul, or St. Peter, or St. John, or of Mary the Mother of Mark, or of Philip's daughters, but in those who, though sent over the earth, have calm faces, and gentle manners, and hearts weaned from the world, and wills subdued; and for their meekness meet with insult, and for their purity with slander, and for their gravity with suspicion, and for their courage with cruelty; yet meet with Christ everywhere—Christ, their all-sufficient, everlasting portion, to make up to them, both here and hereafter, all they suffer, all they dare, for His Name's sake? "Queen of the missions, pray for them."

A PRAYER

WE WILL never give up the hope, the humble belief, that our sweet and gracious Lady will not forget but will recompense him, in royal wise, seven-fold, bringing him and his at length into the Church of the One Saviour, and into the communion of herself and all Saints whom He has redeemed. Amen.

SEEK HIM

WHO can live any time in the world, pleasant as it may seem on first entering it, without discovering that it is a weariness, and that if this life is worth any thing, it is because it is the passage to another? It needs no great enlightment to feel this; it is a self-evident truth to those who have much experience of the world. The only reason why all do not feel it is, that they have not lived long enough to feel it; and those who feel it more than others, have but been thrown into circumstances to feel it more. But while the times wax old, and the colours of the earth fade, and the voice of song is brought low, and all kindreds of the earth can but wail and lament, the sons of God lift up their heads, for their salvation draweth nigh.

Nature fails, the sun shines not, and the moon is dim, the stars fall from heaven, and the foundations of the round world shake; but the Altar's light burns ever brighter; there are sights there which the many cannot see, and all above the tumults of the earth the command is heard to show forth the Lord's death, and the promise that the Lord is coming.

Happy are the people that have these things who, when wearied of the things seen, can turn with good hope to the things unseen; yea, "blessed are the people whose God is the Lord." "Come unto Me," He says, "all ye that labour and are burdened, and I will refresh ye." Rest is better than toil, peace satisfies, and quietness disappoints not. These are sure goods. Such is the calm of the heavenly Jerusalem, which is the mother of us all: and such is their calm worship, the foretaste of heaven, who for a season shut themselves out from the world, and seek Him in invisible Presence, Whom they shall hereafter see face to face.

ETERNAL KINGDOM

AND WHEN Christ comes at last, blessed indeed will be my lot. I have joined myself from the first to the conquering side; I have risked the present against the future, preferring the certainty of eternity to the chance of time; and then my reward will be but beginning when that of the children of this world is come to an end. I shall be numbered among the children of God, and my lot will be among the saints. I pray Thee ever to enlighten the eyes of my understanding that I may belong to the Heavenly Host, not to this world; that I may approach Thee, possess Thee, see Thee, even upon earth. Amen.

I pray Thee by the merits of Thy cross and passion to have mercy on me, on all I love, on all the Church; to pardon me, to give me repentance, and to bestow on me, according to the riches of Thy love, future blessedness in Thy eternal Kingdom. Amen.

God save us all, young and old, from sin, through Jesus Christ. Amen.

ARMOR OF GOD

LET me turn to God with a perfect heart; let me beg of Him that grace which wrought so powerfully in the blessed Apostle, St. Paul; let me put on the whole armor of God, that I may be able to withstand in the evil day, and having done all to stand. Let me be sure that, if I have but the will for great things, I have the power. Let me meditate upon the lives of the Saints in times past, and see how much a resolute unflinching will did for them.

IN ME

LET me aim at God's glory; let it be my daily prayer that God may be glorified in me, whether in my life or in my death, whether in my punishment or in my release, in my pain or in my refreshment, in my toil or in my repose, in my honour or in my dishonour, in my lifting up or in my humiliation.

Let me beware of receiving His grace in vain. When God called Samuel, he answered, "Speak, Lord, for Thy servant heareth."

LOVING FATHER

OH, HARD it is to say this, and to endure to put one's self into God's hands! Yet He is the faithful God, not willingly afflicting the sons of men, but for their good; not chastising us, but as a loving Father; not tempting us, without making a way to escape; not implanting the thorn in our flesh, save to temper the abundance of His revelations.

IN THE DARKNESS

"ALL THINGS are thine, and we have given Thee what we received of Thy hand." (I Par. 29, 14.) If we have had the rain in its season, and the sun shining in its strength, and the fertile ground, it is of Thee. We give back to Thee what came from Thee.

He gives, He takes away. "If we have received good things at the hand of God, why should we not receive evil?" May He not do what He will with His own? May not His sun set as it has risen? and must it not set, if it is to rise again? and must not darkness come first, if there is ever to be morning? and must not the sky be blacker, before it can be brighter? And cannot He, who can do all things, cause a light to arise even in the darkness? "In the night I have remembered Thy Name O Lord, and have kept Thy Law." (Ps. 118, 55.)

GIVEN BACK

AND TIME, and matter, and motion, and force, and the will of man, how vain are they all, except as instruments of the grace of God, blessing them and working with them! How vain are all our pains, our thought, our care, unless God uses them, unless God has inspired them! how worse than fruitless are they, unless directed to His glory, and given back to the Giver. Amen.

PILGRIM

CONSIDER the special prayer which the Lord Himself taught us, as a pattern of all prayer. It consists of seven petitions; three have reference to Almighty God, four to the petitioners; and could any form of words be put together which so well could be called the Prayer of the Pilgrim? We often hear it said, that the true way of serving God is to serve man, as if religion consisted merely in acting well our part in life, not in direct faith, obedience, and worship: how different is the spirit of this prayer! Evil round about him, enemies and persecutors in his path, temptation in prospect, help for the day, sin to be expiated, God's will in his heart, God's Name on his lips, God's kingdom in his hopes; this is the view it gives us of a Christian. What simplicity! What grandeur! and what definiteness! how one and the same, how consistent with all that we read of him elsewhere in Scripture! "Our Father, who art in heaven, etc."

MY PORTION FOREVER

LIFE passes, riches fly away, popularity is fickle, the senses decay, the world changes, friends die. One alone is constant; One alone is true to me; One alone can be true; One alone can be all things to me; One alone can supply my needs; One alone can train me up to my full perfection; One alone can give a meaning to my complex and intricate nature; One alone can give me tune and harmony; One alone can form and possess me. Has He really made me His child? In spite of my sins, He will receive me still, if I seek His face in love unfeigned and holy fear. Let me say with the Psalmist, "Thou art the God of my heart, and the God that is my portion forever." Amen.

INWARD MAN

GOD has graciously willed to bring us to heaven; to practise a heavenly life on earth, certainly, is a thing above earth. It is like trying to execute some high and refined harmony on an insignificant instrument. In attempting it, that instrument would be taxed beyond its powers, and would be sacrificed to great ideas beyond itself. And so, in a certain sense, this life, and our present nature, is sacrificed for heaven and the new creature. Grant, Lord Jesus, that while our outward man perishes, our inward man may be renewed day by day. Amen.

GUIDE ME

LET me beg of my Divine Lord to take to Him His great power, and manifest Himself more and more, and reign both in my heart and in the world. Let me beg of Him to stand by me in trouble, and guide me on my dangerous way. Amen.

FUTURE

SEASONS of peace, indeed, will be vouch-safed to me, and in the most fearful times; but not a life of peace. A reign of temporal peace I can hardly enjoy. Peace and rest are future.

JUDGMENT

MAY GOD raise my heart on high to seek first His kingdom and His justice, that all other things may be added to me! Let what is inward be chief with me, and what is outward be subordinate! Think nothing preferable to a knowledge of myself, true repentance, a resolve to live to God, to die to the world, deep humility, hatred of sin, and of myself as I am a sinner, a clear and habitual view of the coming judgment.

HIS YOKE

TO COME to Christ, is to come after Him; to take up my cross, is to take upon me His yoke; and though He calls this an easy yoke, yet it is easy because it is His yoke, and He makes it easy; still it does not cease to be a yoke, and it is troublesome and distressing because it is a yoke. We adore Thee, O Christ, and we bless Thee, etc.

A CROWN

WHATEVER be my necessary trial, He will bring me through it—through the deep waters, through the thick darkness— as He guided and guarded the blessed Apostle; till I in turn, whatever be my past sins, shall be able to say, like him, "I have fought a good fight, I have finished my course, I have kept the faith. As to the rest, there is laid up for me a crown of justice, which the Lord the just judge will render to me in that day."

THE CHURCH

THE CHURCH, like her Divine Author, regards, consults for, labors for, the individual soul; she looks at the souls for whom Christ died, and who are made over to her; and her one object, for which everything is sacrificed—appearances, reputation, worldly triumph—is to acquit herself well of this most awful responsibility. Her one duty is to bring forward the elect to salvation, and to make them as many as she can:—to take offences out of their path, to warn them of sin, to rescue them from evil, to convert them, to teach them, to feed them, to protect them, and to perfect them. . . She overlooks everything in comparison of the immortal soul. Good and evil to her are not lights and shades passing over the surface of society, but living powers, springing from the depths of the heart. Actions, in her sight, are not mere outward deeds and words, committed by hand or tongue, and manifested in effects over a range of influence wider or narrower, as the case may be; but they are the thoughts, the desires, the purposes, of the solitary responsible spirit.

TIME

MEN on their death-beds have declared, that no one could form a right idea of the value of time till he came to die; but if this has truth in it, how much more truly can it be said after death! What an estimate shall I form of time while I am being judged! Yes, it is I—all this, I repeat, belongs to me most intimately. It is not to be looked at as a picture, as a man might read a light book in a leisure hour. All must die, the youngest, the healthiest, the most thoughtless; I must be thus unnaturally torn in two, soul from body; to be united again and made happy for ever!

THANKS TO THE CRUCIFIED

Now I bid you consider that that Face, so ruthlessly smitten, was the Face of God Himself; the Brows bloody with the thorns, the sacred Body exposed to view and lacerated with the scourge, the Hands nailed to the Cross, and, afterwards, the Side pierced with the spear; it was the Blood, and the sacred Flesh, and the Hands, and the Temples, and the Side, and the Feet of God Himself, which the frenzied multitude then gazed upon.

DELUSIONS

IT IS not Thy loss if I love Thee not, it is my loss. Thou art All-blessed, whatever becomes of me. Thou art not less blessed because I am far from Thee. It is I who am not blessed, except as I approach Thee, except as I am like Thee, in the day in which Thou will come from Heaven. I have made pride, or selfishness, or the carnal mind, my standard of perfection and truth; my eyes have grown dim, and my heart gross, as regards the true Light of men, and the Glory of the Eternal Father. May Thou Thyself save me from my self-delusions, whatever they are, and enable me to give up this world, that I may gain the next;—and to rejoice in Thee, who had no home of Thy own, no place to lay Thy head, who were poor and lowly, and despised and rejected, and tormented and slain! Amen.

TILL CHRIST COMES

RESIGNATION is a more blessed frame of mind than sanguine hope of present success, because it is the truer, and the more consistent with our fallen state of being, and the more improving to our hearts; and because it is that for which the most eminent servants of God have been conspicuous. To expect great effects from our exertions for religious objects is natural indeed, and innocent, but it arises from inexperience of the kind of work we have to do,—to change the heart and will of man. It is a far nobler frame of mind, to labour, not with the hope of seeing the fruit of our labour, but for conscience's sake, as a matter of duty; and again, in faith, trusting good *will* be done, though we see it not.

Even in the successes of the first Christian teachers, the Apostles, the same rule is observed. After all the great works God enabled them to accomplish, they confessed before their death that what they experienced, and what they saw before them, was reverse and calamity, and that the fruit of their labour would not be seen, till Christ came to open the books and collect His saints from the four corners of the earth. "Evil men and seducers shall wax worse and worse, deceiving and being deceived," is the testimony of St. Peter, St. Paul, St. John and St. Jude.

SAVE ME

IN ALL circumstances, of joy or sorrow, hope or fear, let me aim at having Thee in my inmost heart; let me have no secret apart from Thee. Let me acknowledge Thee as enthroned within me at the very springs of thought and affection. Let me submit myself to Thy guidance and sovereign direction; let me come to Thee that Thou mayest forgive me, cleanse me, change me, guide me, and save me. Amen.

Let me pray Thee that at the Last Day, when all veils are removed, I may be found among those who were ever spoken against in their generation, eternally honored afterwards; who with Enoch and Noah and Abraham and Moses and Joshua and Phineas and Elias and the Baptist and St. Paul ("I had patience and have endured for His Name's sake and I have not fainted,") have watched in all things, done the work of a Christian, fought a good fight, finished their course, kept the faith. Amen.

HOW LITTLE

"LORD, remember me when Thou shalt come into Thy Kingdom." Such was the prayer of the penitent thief on the cross, such must be our prayer. Who can do us any good, but He, who shall also be our Judge? When shocking thoughts about ourselves come across us and afflict us, "Remember me," this is all we have to say. We have "no work, nor reason, nor wisdom, nor knowledge" of our own, to better ourselves withal. We can say nothing to God in defence of ourselves, we can but acknowledge that we are grievous sinners, and addressing Him as suppliants, merely beg Him to bear us in mind in mercy, for His Son's sake to do us some favor, not according to our deserts, but for the love of Christ. We are forced out of ourselves by the very necessity of our condition.

To whom should we go? Who can do us any good, but He who was born into this world as our Saviour, was bruised for our iniquities, and rose again for our salvation? Even though we have served Him from our youth up, though after His pattern we have grown, as far as mere man can grow, in wisdom as we grew in stature, though we ever have had tender hearts, and a mortified will, and a conscientious temper, and an obedient spirit; yet, at the very best, how much have we left undone, how much done which ought to be otherwise! What He can do for our nature, in the way of sanctifying it, we know in the case of His saints. But for ourselves, we know full well that much as we may have attempted, we have done very little; the more we attempt, the more clearly we see how little we have hitherto attempted.

REJOICE ALWAYS

THOSE whom Christ saves are they who at once attempt to save themselves, yet are fearful of saving themselves; who aim to do all, and confess they do nought; who are all love, and all fear; who are the most holy, and yet confess themselves the most sinful; who ever seek to please Him, yet feel they never can; who are full of good works, yet of works of penance. All this seems a contradiction to the natural man, but it is not so to those whom Christ enlightens. They understand in proportion to their illumination, that it is possible to work out their salvation, yet to have it wrought out for them, to fear and tremble at the thought of judgment, yet to rejoice always in the Lord, and hope and pray for His coming. Amen.

NO SIN

A HOLY MAN is by nature subject to sin equally with others; but he is holy because he subdues, tramples on, chains up, imprisons, puts out of the way temptations of sin, and is ruled by religious and spiritual motives. Of Christ was it said that He "did no sin, neither was guile found in His mouth." The prince of this world came and found no sin in Him. He had no root of sin in His heart; He was not born in Adam's sin. Far different are we! He was thus pure, because He was the Son of God and born of a Virgin.

WITHOUT DRAWBACK

IN THIS LIFE, even to the end, there will be enough evil in us to humble us; even to the end, the holiest men have remains and stains of sin which they would fain get rid of, if they could, and which keep this life from being to them, for all God's grace, a heaven upon earth. No, the Christian life is but a shadow of heaven. Its festal and holy days are but shadows of eternity. But hereafter it will be otherwise.

In heaven, sin will be utterly destroyed in every soul. We shall have no earthly wishes, no tendencies to disobedience or irreligion, no love of the world, or the flesh, to draw us off from supreme devotion to God. We shall have Our Saviour's holiness fulfilled in us, and be able to love God without drawback or infirmity. "Thy Kingdom come."

WITH CHRIST

WHAT a time will that be, when all will be perfected in us which at present is but feebly begun! Then we shall see how the Angels worship God. We shall see the calmness, the intenseness, the purity, of their worship. We shall see that awful sight, the Throne of God, and the Seraphim before and around it, crying, "Holy!" We attempt now to join with what there is performed, as in the beginning, and ever shall be. In the Te Deum, day by day we say, "Holy, Holy, Holy Lord God of Sabaoth." In the Creed, we recount God's mercies to us sinners. And we say and sing Psalms and Hymns, to come as near heaven as we can.

May these attempts of mine be blest by Almighty God, to prepare me for Him! May they be not dead forms, but living prayers, living with life from God the Holy Ghost, in me who am dead to sin and who live with Christ! Amen.

TO LIVE

I COME to God, and beg of Him grace to devote myself to Him. Beg of Him the will to follow Him; beg of Him the power to obey Him. O how comfortable, pleasant, sweet, soothing and satisfying is it to lead a holy life,—the life of Angels! It is difficult at first; but with God's grace, all things are possible. O how pleasant to have done with sin! how good and joyful to flee temptation and to resist evil! How meet, and worthy, and fitting, and right, to die unto sin, and to live unto holiness! Amen.

LET me then think of this, and if a religious life is pleasant here, in spite of the old Adam interrupting the pleasure and defiling us, what a glorious day it will be, if it is granted to us hereafter to enter into the Kingdom of Heaven! None of us, even the holiest, can guess *how* happy we shall be; for St. John says, "It hath not appeared what we shall be"; and St. Paul, "Now we see in a glass in a dark manner, but then face to face." Yet in proportion to our present holiness and virtue, we have some faint ideas of what will then be our blessedness. And in Scripture various descriptions of heaven are given us, in order to arrest, encourage and humble us.

We are told, that the Angels of God are very bright, and clad in white robes. The Saints and Martyrs too are clad in white robes, with palms in their hands; and they sing praises unto Him that sitteth upon the Throne, and to the Lamb. When our Lord was transfigured, He showed us what Heaven is. His raiment became white as snow, white and glistening. Again, at one time He appeared to St. John, and then, "His head and His hairs were white as white wool, and as snow, and his eyes were as a flame of fire; and His feet like unto fine brass, as in a burning furnace; and His face was as the sun shineth in his power."

And what Christ is, such do His saints become hereafter. Here below they are clad in a garment of sinful flesh; but when the end comes, and they rise from the grave, they shall inherit glory, and shall be ever young and ever shining. In that day, all men will see and be convinced, even bad men, that God's servants are really happy, and only they.

AT THE LAST

LET me think of all this and rouse myself, and run forward with a good courage on my way towards Heaven. Be not weary in well-doing, for in due season I shall reap, if I faint not. Strive to enter in at the strait gate. Strive to get holier and holier every day, that I may be worthy to stand before the Son of Man. Pray God to teach me His will, and to lead me forth in the right way, because of my enemies. Submit myself to His guidance, and I shall have comfort given me, according to my day, and peace at the last. Amen.

UPON CHRIST

FAR be it from us, soldiers of Christ, to perplex ourselves with this world, who are making our way towards the world to come. "No man being a soldier to God entangleth himself with the secular businesses, that he may please Him to whom he hath engaged himself. For he also that striveth for the mastery, is not crowned, except he strive lawfully." This is St. Paul's rule, as has already been referred to: accordingly, in another place, he bears witness of himself that he "died daily." Day by day he got more and more dead to this world; he had fewer ties to earth, a larger treasure in heaven.

Now let us not think that it is over-difficult to imitate him, though we be not Apostles, nor are called to any extraordinary work, nor are enriched with any miraculous gifts: he would have all men like himself, and all may be like him, according to their place and measure of grace. If we would be followers of the great Apostle, first let us fix our eyes upon Christ our Saviour; consider the splendour and glory of His holiness, and try to love it.

REMIND US

AND IT IS God's usual mode of dealing with us, in mercy to send the shadow before the substance, that we may take comfort in what is to be, before it comes. Thus our Lord before His Passion rode into Jerusalem in triumph, with the multitudes crying Hosanna, and strewing His road with palm branches and their garments. This was but a vain and hollow pageant, nor did Our Lord take pleasure in it. It was a shadow which stayed not, but flitted away. It could not be more than a shadow, for the Passion had not been undergone by which His true triumph was wrought out. He could not enter into His glory before He had first suffered. He could not take pleasure in this semblance of it, knowing that it was unreal.

Yet that first shadowy triumph was the omen and presage of the true victory to come, when He had overcome the sharpness of death. And we commemorate this figurative triumph on the last Sunday in Lent, to cheer us in the sorrow of the week that follows, and to remind us of the true joy which comes with Easter-Day.

ALL THINGS

AND SO, too, as regards this world, with all its enjoyments, yet disappointments. Let us not trust, let us not give our hearts to it; let us not begin with it. Let us begin with His Cross and the humiliation to which it leads. Let us first be drawn to Him who is lifted up, that so He may, with Himself, freely give us all things. Let us seek the Kingdom of God and His justice, and then all those things of this world will be added to us.

A SHADOW

THEY alone are able to enjoy this world, who begin with the world unseen. They alone enjoy it, who have first abstained from it. They alone can truly feast, who have first fasted; they alone are able to use the world, who have learned not to abuse it; they alone inherit it; who take it as a shadow of the world to come, and who for that world to come relinquish it.

St. Paul went through trials of every kind, and this was their issue, to let him into the feelings, and thereby introduce him to the hearts of high and low. . . . He knew how to persuade, for he knew where to lay the perplexity; he knew how to console, for he knew the sorrow. His spirit within him was as some delicate instrument, which, as the weather changed about him, as the atmosphere was moist or dry, hot or cold, accurately marked all its variations, and guided him what to do.

Let us look upon Him who was lifted up that He might draw us near to Him, and, by being drawn one and all to Him, let us be drawn to each other, so that we may understand and feel that He has redeemed us one and all, and that, unless we love one another, we cannot really have love to Him who laid down His life for us.

There was a virtue in His death, which there could be in no other, for He was God.

LEAVE HIM?

TRUST ME, rather than the world, when I tell you, that it is no difficult thing for a Catholic to believe. He has received a gift which makes faith easy; it is not without an effort, a miserable effort, that any one who has received that gift, unlearns to believe. He does violence to his mind, not in exercising, but in withholding his faith. When objections occur to him, which they may easily do if he lives in the world, they are as odious and unwelcome to him as impure thoughts are to the virtuous. He does certainly shrink from them, he flings them away from him, but why? not in the first instance, because they are dangerous, but because they are cruel and base. His loving Lord has done everything for him, and has He deserved such a return? He has poured on us His grace, He has been with us in our perplexities, He has forgiven us our sins, He has satisfied our reason, He has made faith easy, He has given us His Saints, He shows before us day by day His own Passion; why should I leave Him? What has he ever done to me but good?

[200]

III

THE LIFE

Narrow, indeed, is the way of life, but infinite is His love and power who is with us to guide us along it.

ABBA, FATHER

BY THE coming of the Holy Ghost, all guilt and pollution are burned away as by fire, the devil is driven forth, sin, original and actual, is forgiven, and the whole man is consecrated to God. As the potter molds the clay, so He impresses the Divine image on us members of the household of God. Being then the sons of God, and one with Him, our souls mount up and cry to Him continually, "Abba, Father."

THE LORD'S PRAYER

I BEGIN it by using my privilege of calling on Almighty God in express words as "Our Father." I proceed, according to this beginning, in that waiting, trusting, adoring, resigned temper which children ought to feel; looking towards Him, rather than thinking of myself; zealous for His honor rather than fearful about my safety; resting in His present help, not with eyes timorously glancing towards the future. His name, His kingdom, His will, are the great objects for the Christian to contemplate and make his portion, being stable and serene, and complete in Him, as beseems one who has the gracious presence of His Spirit within him. And, when I go on to think of myself, I pray, that I may be enabled to have towards myself, a spirit of forgiveness and loving-kindness, thinking of self as little as may be. And if I have at times special comfortings from the Spirit, I am silent, and ponder it as choice encouragement to my soul, meaning something, but I know not how much. **Our Father, who art in heaven, etc.**

HIS FULNESS

CHRIST came to make a new world. He came into the world to regenerate it in Himself, to make a new beginning, to be the beginning of the creation of God, to gather together in one, and recapitulate all things in Himself. The rays of His glory were scattered through the world; one state of life had some of them, another others. The world was like some fair mirror, broken in pieces, and giving back no one uniform image of its Maker. But He came to combine what was dissipated, to recast what was shattered, in Himself. He began all excellence, and of His fulness have all we received.

MYRRH ALSO

WHEN He came, a Child was born, a Son given, and yet He was Wonderful, Counsellor, the Mighty God, the Everlasting Father, the Prince of Peace. Angels heralded a Saviour, a Christ, a Lord; but withal, He was "born in Bethlehem," and was "lying in a manger." Eastern sages brought Him gold, for that He was a King, frankincense as to a God; but on the other hand myrrh also, in token of a coming death and burial. At the last, He bore witness to the truth before Pilate as a Prophet, suffered on the Cross as our Priest, while He was also "Jesus of Nazareth, the King of the Jews."

Such too is the characteristic of Catholicity; not the highest in rank, not the meanest, not the most refined, not the rudest, is beyond the influence of the Church. Every class is among her children.

HIS LIKENESS

AND SO His apostles after Him, and in His likeness, were kings, yet without the pomp; soldiers, yet with no blood but their own; teachers, yet withal their own disciples, acting out in their own persons, and by their own labours, their own precepts.

HIS SHADOWS

AND SO, in after-times, those Saints and Fathers to whom we look up, have joined these three offices together. Great doctors they have been, but not mere philosophers or men of letters, but noble-minded rulers of the churches; nor only so, but preachers, missionaries, monastic brethren, confessors, and martyrs. This is the glory of the Church, to speak, to do, and to suffer, with that grace which Christ brought and diffused abroad. And it has run down even to the skirts of her clothing. Not the few and the conspicuous alone, but all her children, high and low, who walk worthy of her and her Divine Lord, will be shadows of Him.

PROPHET PRINCE KING

ALL of us are bound according to our opportunities,—first to learn the truth; and moreover, we must not only know, but we must impart our knowledge. Nor only so, but next we must bear witness to the truth. We must not be afraid of the frowns of anger of the world, or mind its ridicule. If so be, we must be willing to suffer for the truth. This was that new thing that Christ brought into the world, a heavenly doctrine, a system of holy and supernatural truths, which are to be received and transmitted, for He is our Prophet; maintained even unto suffering after His pattern, who is our Priest, and obeyed, for He is our King. Our Father, who art in heaven, etc.

CONTEMPLATING GOD

THE THOUGHT of God, and nothing short of it, is the happiness of man. He alone is sufficient for the heart who made it. To none besides can the whole heart in all its thoughts and feelings be unlocked and subjected. He who is infinite can alone be its measure; He alone can answer to the mysterious assemblage of feelings and thoughts which it has within it. St. Paul seems to delight in the continual laying open of his heart to God, and submitting it to His scrutiny and waiting for His Presence upon it: with all good conscience before God until this present day, and while contemplating God, to dwell on the thought of God's contemplating him.

Be, Thou alone, sufficient for my heart, Thou, who hast made it. Amen.

Thou didst mean me to be simple, to think no evil, yet a thousand associations, bad, trifling or unworthy, attend my every thought. Thou hast purchased for me what I lost, in Adam, my garment of grace. Bid me and enable me to become as little children, for of such is the kingdom of heaven. Amen.

THY SECOND COMING

I SHOULD understand that I am called to be a stranger and pilgrim upon the earth and that my worldly lot and wordly goods are a sort of accident of my existence, and that I really have no property, though human law guarantees property to me. Let me stand upon my watch, let me watch to see what will be said to me; that I may answer hopefully to Thee. Amen.

I watch with Christ if I, while I look on to the future, look back on the past, and do not so contemplate what my Saviour has purchased for me, as to forget what He has suffered for me. I watch with Christ, if I ever commemorate and renew in my own person Christ's Cross and Agony, and gladly take up that mantle of affliction which Christ wore here, and left behind Him when He ascended. If I suffer with Him, that I may be also glorified with Him.

This then is to watch; to be detached from what is present, and to live in what is unseen; to live in the thought of Christ as He came once, and as He will come again; to desire Thy second coming, from my affectionate and grateful remembrance of Thy first. "I believe in God—to judge the living and the dead."

ALL IN ONE

DAY and night was he parched with heat and with frost. In the day the drought consumed him and the frost consumed him by night Jacob tells us, and his sleep departed from his eyes; and read we not of One Whose wont it was to rise a long while before day, and continue in prayer to God? Who passed nights in the mountain, or on the sea? Who dwelt forty days in the wilderness? Who in the evening and night of His passion was forlorn in the bleak garden, or stripped and bleeding in the cold judgment hall? Thou didst fulfill all types, the lowly Jacob, the wise Moses, the heroic David, Thou, Who wast all in one Priest, Prophet and King, have mercy on me. Amen.

Seek I great things? I must seek them where they really are to be found, and in the way in which they are to be found; I must seek them as He hast sought them before me, who came into the world to enable me to gain them. I must be willing to give up present hope for future enjoyment, this world for the unseen.

I pray God to give me this great and

precious gift; rid myself of selfish motives, self-conceit, and vanity, littleness, envying, grudgings, meannesses; turn from all cowardly, low, miserable ways, obeying St. Paul's "Do all things without murmuring or criticising . . . faultless 'in the midst of an age that is crooked and perverse' . . . not for nothing have I run my race, not for nothing spent my toil." Amen.

FOLLOW HIM

TO GET UP day after day to the same employments, and to feel happy in them, is the great lesson of the Gospel. The Christian temper is in its perfect and peculiar enjoyment when engaged in that ordinary, unvaried course of duties which God assigns, and which the world calls dull and tiresome. In proportion to the strength of the distractions which surround me is my blessedness and my praise, if I am enabled amid the waves of the sea and the great wisdom of their traffic to hear Christ's voice, to take up my cross, and follow Thee. Amen.

WATCH FOR HIM

WHAT treasure can equal time? It is the seed of eternity yet I suffer myself to go on, year after year, hardly using it at all in God's service. . . . I try how little I can safely give to religion. . . . I sit down to eat, and drink, and rise up to play, when time is hurrying on and judgment coming. . . . May I have expectant ears, and watch for Christ. Amen.

May I then come before Thee as now I come to pray—with profound abasement, with awe, with self-renunciation, still as relying upon Thy Holy Spirit whom Thou hast given me, with my faculties about me, with a collected and determined mind, and with hope. Amen.

CLOSE TO THEE

LET us not be content with ourselves; let us pray for the gift of watchful ears and a willing heart. He calls us each in His own way. Let us not make our own hearts our home, or this world our home; let us look out for a better country, that is, an heavenly. Let us look out for Him Who alone can guide us to that better country; let us

call heaven our home, and this life a pilgrimage; let us view ourselves as sheep in
the trackless desert, who, unless they follow the shepherd, will be sure to lose
themselves, sure to fall in with the wolf.
We are safe while we keep close to Thee
and under Thy eye; but if we suffer Satan
to gain an advantage over us, woe to us!

REALITIES

THE CHURCH professes to judge after
the judgment of the Almighty; and it cannot be imprudent or impolitical to bring
this out clearly and boldly. His judgment
is not as man's: "I judge not according to
the look of man." He says, "for man seeth
those things which appear, but the Lord
beholdeth the heart." The Church aims at
realities, the world at decencies; she dis-
penses with a complete work, so she can
but make a thorough one. Provided she
can do for the soul what is necessary, if she
can but pull the brands out of the burning, if she can but extract the poisonous
root which is the death of the soul, and expel the disease, she is content, though she
leaves in it lesser maladies, little as she
sympathizes with them.

WE MIGHT KNOW

EVERY holy rite of the law did Christ go
through for our sakes. And so too did He
live through all states of man's life up to a
perfect man, infancy, childhood, boyhood,
youth, maturity, that He might be a pattern of them all. And so too did He take
man's nature on Him, body, and soul, and
reason, that He might sanctify it wholly.
And therefore in like manner did He
unite in Himself, and renew, and give us
back in Him, the principal lots or states in
which we find ourselves,—suffering, that
we might know how to suffer; laboring,
that we might know how to labor; and
teaching, that we might know how to
teach.

Thus, when our Lord came on earth
in our nature, He combined together offices and duties most dissimilar. He suffered, yet He triumphed. He thought and
spoke, yet He acted. He was humble and
despised, yet He was a teacher. He has at
once a life of hardship like the shepherds,
yet is wise and royal as the eastern sages
who came to do honor to His birth.

May I seek the grace of a cheerful

heart, an even temper, sweetness, gentleness and brightness of mind, as walking in
Thy light and by Thy grace. Amen.

EARTHEN VESSELS

AND further this may be observed, that
when Christ had thus given a pattern in
Himself of such contrary modes of life,
and their contrary excellences, all in one,
He did not, on His going away, altogether
withdraw the wonderful spectacle; but He
left behind Him those who should take
His place, a priestly order, who are His
representatives and instruments; and they,
though earthen vessels, show forth according to their measure these three charac-
ters,—the prophetical, priestly, and regal,
combining in themselves qualities and
functions which, except under the Gospel,
are almost incompatible the one with the
other. He consecrated His Apostles to
suffer, when He said, "My chalice indeed
you shall drink"; to teach, when He said,
"the Paraclete, the Holy Ghost, He will
teach you all things"; and to rule, when
He said to them, "I dispose you as My
Father has disposed Me a kingdom, that

ye may eat and drink at My table in My Kingdom; and may sit upon thrones, judging the twelve tribes of Israel."

Let me pray Thee to give me the spirit of ever-abundant, ever-springing love, which overpowers and sweeps away the vexations of life by its own richness and strength, and which above all things unites me to Thee who art the fountain and the center of all mercy, loving kindness and joy. Amen.

KINGLY POWER

HOW inviting the sovereignty of Christ! Born, not in golden chambers, but in a cave of the earth, surrounded with brute cattle, laid in a manger; then bred up as the carpenter's son; then He displayed Himself as the King of Saints, still without a place to lay His head, and dying on the Cross a malefactor's death. He was not a king without being a sufferer too. And so in like manner His followers after Him. He washed His brethren's feet, and He bade them in turn do the like. He told them that he that will be the first among them, shall be their servant, "even as the

Son of Man is not come to be ministered unto, but to minister, and to give His life a redemption for many." He warned them that they should receive "houses and lands, with persecutions." Such is the kingly power of Christ,—reached through humiliation, exercised in mortification.

Thou hast brought us light and life, and wouldst have us put off self and follow Thee, who didst know no sin. Worship and service make up the Angels' blessedness; and such is our blessedness in proportion as we approach them. Like them may I cry, Holy, Holy, Holy, and do Thy bidding. Amen.

VISIT ME

ADVENT and Lent are special seasons for cleansing myself from all sin; seasons for chastened hearts and religious eyes; for severe thoughts, and austere resolves, and charitable deeds; a season for remembering what I am and what I shall be.

Let me go out to meet Thee with contrite and expectant heart; and though Thou dost delay Thy coming, let me watch for Thee in the cold and dreariness which must one day have an end. Attend Thy summons I must, at any rate, when Thou dost strip me of the body; let me anticipate, by a voluntary act, what will one day come on me of necessity.

Let me wait for Thee solemnly, fearfully, hopefully, patiently, obediently, let me be resigned to Thy will, while active in good works. Let me pray Thee ever, to remember me when Thou dost come into Thy kingdom; to remember all my friends; to remember my enemies; and to visit me according to Thy mercy here, that Thou mayest reward me according to Thy justice hereafter. Amen.

HIS DEATH

IT IS the death of the Eternal Word of God made flesh, which is my great lesson how to think and how to speak of this world. His Cross has put its due value upon everything which I see, upon all fortunes, all advantages, all ranks, all dignities, all pleasures; upon the lust of the eyes, and the pride of life. It has set a price upon the excitements, the rivalries, the hopes, the fears, the desires, the efforts, the triumphs of mortal man. It has given a meaning to the various, shifting course, the trials, the temptations, the sufferings, of his earthly state. It has brought together and made consistent all that seemed discordant and aimless. It has taught me how to live, how to use this world, what to expect, what to desire, what to hope. It is the tone into which all the strains of this world's music are ultimately to be resolved.

Thus in the Cross, and Him who hung upon it, all things meet; all things subserve it, all things need it. It is their centre and their interpretation. For He was lifted up upon it, that He might draw all men and all things unto Him. Amen.

PENITENCE

TRUE penitence is that which never comes to an end; and true penance is that which lasts as long as penitence.

O my God, I am heartily sorry for ever having offended Thee, who created me, who redeemed me on Thy holy Cross. Amen.

FOUNDATION

THERE are many persons who proceed a little way in religion, and then stop short. God keep me from choking the good seed, which else would come to perfection! Let me exercise myself in these good works, which both reverse the evil that is past, and lay up a good foundation for me in the world to come. Amen.

CONTINUANCE

LET me turn from shadows of all things, —shadows of sense, or shadows of argument and disputation, or shadows addressed to my imagination and tastes. Let me attempt, through God's grace, to advance and sanctify the inward man. I cannot be wrong here. Whatever is right, whatever is wrong, in this perplexing world, I must be right in doing justly, in living mercy, in walking humbly with our God; in denying my will, in ruling my tongue, in softening and sweetening my temper, in mortifying my lusts; in learning patience, meekness, purity, forgiveness of injuries, and continuance in well-doing. Amen.

WHEN the Son of Man, the First-born of the creation of God, came to the evening of His mortal life, He parted with His disciples at a feast. He had borne "the burden and heat of the day"; yet, when "wearied with His journey," He had but stopped at the well's side, and asked a draught of water for His thirst; for He had "meat to eat which" others "knew not of." His meat was "to do the will of Him that sent Him, and to perfect His work"; "I must work the works of Him that sent Me," said He, "whilst it is day; the night cometh, when no man can work."

Thus passed the season of His ministry; and if at any time He feasted with Pharisee or Publican, it was in order that He might do the work of God more strenuously. But "when it was evening, He sat down with His twelve disciples! And He said unto them: With desire, I have desired to eat this Pasch with you, before I suffer." He was about to suffer more than man had ever suffered or shall suffer. But there is nothing gloomy, churlish, violent, or selfish in His grief; it is tender, affectionate, social. He calls His friends around Him, though He was as Job among the ashes; He bids them stay by Him, and see Him suffer; He desires their sympathy; He takes refuge in their love. He first feasted them, and sung a hymn with them, and washed their feet; and when His long trial began, He beheld them and kept them in His presence, till they in terror shrank from it. Yet, on Mary and St. John, His Virgin Mother and His Virgin Disciple, who remained, His eyes still rested; and in St. Peter, who was denying Him in the distance, His sudden glance wrought a deep repentance. O wonderful pattern, the type of all trial and of all duty under it! "Our Father, who art in heaven."

CHARITY

WHAT is man, what are we, what am I, that the Son of God should be so mindful of me? What am I that He should have raised me who from my youth up have been a transgressor, and should Himself dwell personally in this very heart of mine, making me His temple? What am I that God the Holy Ghost should enter into me, and draw up my thoughts heavenward with plaints unutterable?

Thou art the fruitful Vine, and the rich Olive Tree upon and out of which all Saints, though wild and barren by nature, grow, that they may bring forth fruit unto God. Let me feel tenderly affectioned towards all whom Thou hast made Thy own by Baptism. Let me sympathize with them, and have kind thoughts towards them, and be warm-hearted, and loving, and simple-minded, and gentle-tempered towards them, and consult for their good, and pray for their growth in faith and holiness. For Thou art charity, and if we love one another, Thou dost abide in us and Thy love is perfected in us.

God grant to us all, out of the superabundant treasures of His grace, such a spirit of Charity. Amen.

WHO MADE IT

OUR REAL and true bliss lies in the possession of those objects on which our hearts may rest and be satisfied. Now, if this be so, here is at once a reason for saying that the thought of God, and nothing short of it, is the happiness of man; for though there is much besides to serve as subject of knowledge, or motive for action, or means of excitement, yet the affections require a something more vast and more enduring than anything created. What is novel and sudden excites but does not influence; what is pleasurable or useful raises no awe; self moves no reverence, and mere knowledge kindles no love. God alone is sufficient for the heart who made it.

ALL VANISH

DO not all men die? are they not taken from us? are they not as uncertain as the grass of the field? We do not give our hearts to things irrational, because these have no permanence in them. We do not place our affections in sun, moon, and stars, or this rich and fair earth, because all things material come to nought, and vanish like day and night.

Man, too, though he has an intelligence within him, yet in his best estate he is altogether vanity. If our happiness consists in our affections being employed and recompensed, "man that is born of a woman" cannot be our happiness; for how can he stay another, who "continueth not in one stay" himself?

THINGS ABOVE

LET me then labour to be really in earnest, and to view things in the way in which God views them. Then it will be but a little thing to give up the world; only an easy thing to reconcile the mind to what at first it shrinks from. Let me turn my mind heavenward; let me set my thoughts on things above, and in His own time God will set my affections there also. All will in time become natural to me, which at present I do but own to be good and true. I shall covet what at present I do but admire.

TO PERFECT

LET the time past suffice me to have followed my own will; let me desire to form part of that glorious company of Apostles and Prophets, of whom I read in Scripture. Let me cast in my lot with them, and desire to be gathered together under their feet. Let me beg of God to employ me, let me try to obtain a spirit of perfect self-surrender to Him, and an indifference to one thing above another in this world, so that I may be ready to follow His call whenever it comes to me. Thus shall I best employ myself till His voice is heard, patiently preparing for it by meditation, and looking for Him to perfect what I trust His own grace has begun in me. Amen.

THY CROSS

JESUS said to Martha, "Believest thou this?" Wherever there is a heart to answer, "Lord, I believe," there Christ is present. There, Lord, Thou vouchsafest to stand, though unseen—whether over the bed of death or over the grave; whether we ourselves are sinking or those who are dear to us.

Blessed be Thy name! We are as certain, through Thy grace, that Thou art standing over us in love, as though we saw Thee. We will not, after our experience of Lazarus's history, doubt an instant that Thou art thoughtful about us. We will never complain at the course of Thy providence. We beg of Thee an increase of faith, a more understanding view of the mystery of Thy Cross, of the virtue of it. Thou wilt never put upon us more than we can bear, never afflict Thy brethren with any woe except for our own highest benefit. Amen.

May Thou lead me on evermore in the narrow way, who art the One Aid of all that need, the Helper of all that flee to Thee for succor, the Life of them that believe, and the Resurrection of the dead! Amen.

THY JUSTICE

I BEG of Thee to work all repentance and all amendment in me, for I can do nothing of myself; to enable me to hate sin truly, and confess it honestly, and deprecate Thy wrath continually, and to undo its effects diligently, and to bear Thy judgments cheerfully and manfully.

I beg of Thee the spirit of Faith and Hope that I may not repine or despond, or account Thee a hard master; that I may learn lovingly to adore the hand that afflicts me and, as it is said, to kiss the rod, however sharply or long it smites me; that I may look on to the end of all things, which will not tarry, and to Thy coming which will at length save me, and not faint on the rough·way, nor toss upon my couch of thorns; that I may make the words of the prophet my own, which express all that sinners, repentant and suffering, should feel towards Thee: "I will bear the wrath of the Lord, because I have sinned against Him: He will bring me forth into the light, I shall behold His justice."

Thou knowest that I desire to love nothing but Thee, and to trust in nothing but the Cross of Christ, through which I hope to receive its merits, my only effectual help in the day of account. Amen.

THY PROMISE

I WILL sing and praise Thy name. When two or three are gathered together, an interior temple, a holy shrine is formed for them, which nothing without can destroy. Nor will I forget my past sins, because Thou dost allow me peace and joy in spite of them. I will remember them that Thou mayest not remember them; I will repent of them again and again, that Thou mayest forgive them; I will rejoice in the punishment of them if Thou dost punish, thinking it better to be punished in this life than in the next; and if not yet punished, I will be prepared for it. Thou wilt give me grace according to my day, according to Thy gracious promise: "Fear not for I have redeemed Thee, and called thee by thy name; thou art mine." Amen.

I praise Thee, worship Thee, sing to Thee, thank Thee, confess to Thee, give myself up to Thee and ask Thy blessing.

Let me be content with nothing short of perfection; exert myself day by day to grow in knowledge of Thee, in Thy grace; that, thus, I may at length attain to Thy presence, O Almighty God. Amen.

CONFIDENCE

THE ABSENCE of a vigilant walk, of exact conscientiousness in all things, of an earnest and vigorous warfare against my spiritual enemies, in a word, of strictness, this is what obscures my peace and joy. Strictness is the condition of rejoicing.

The Christian is a soldier; I may have many falls; these need not hinder my joy in my Saviour; I must be humbled indeed, but not downcast; it does not prove I am not fighting; I have enemies within and without me, I have the remains of a fallen nature. These avail not to disturb the tranquillity and the intensity of the confidence with which I gaze upon Thy Divine Majesty. Amen.

PERSONAL GOOD

LET me ever anxiously remember that affliction is sent for my own personal good also. Let me fear, lest, after I have ministered to others, I myself should be a castaway; let my gentleness, consideration, and patience which are so soothing to them never be separated from that inward faith and strict conscientiousness which alone unites me to Christ;—lest, in spite of all the good I may do to others, yet I should have some secret fault, some unresisted selfishness within me, which separates me from Him. Let me pray Him who sends me trial, to send me a pure heart and intention wherewith to bear it. Amen.

PLEASE HIM

IT IS the characteristic of St. Paul, as manifested to us in his Epistles, to live in the sight of Him who searcheth the reins and the heart, to love to place himself before Him, and while contemplating God, to dwell on the thought of God's contemplating him. And, it may be, this is something of the Apostle's meaning, when he speaks of the witness of the Spirit. Perhaps he is speaking of that satisfaction and rest which the soul experiences in proportion as it is able to surrender itself wholly to God, and to have no desire, no aim, but to please Him.

Our happiness consists in the thought of God. Such contemplation is alone capable of accompanying the mind always and everywhere, for God alone can be always and everywhere present. What is commonly said about the happiness of a good conscience, when we examine the force of our words, but to be ever reminded of God by our own hearts, to have our hearts in such a state as to be led thereby to look up to Him, and to desire His eyes to be upon us through the day?

OUR JUDGE

THERE is One who is justified in His sayings, and clear when He judgeth. Our worldly philosophy and our well-devised pleadings will profit nothing at a day when the heaven shall depart as a scroll is rolled together, and all who are not clad in the wedding-garment of faith and love will be speechless. Surely it is high time for us to wake out of sleep, to chase from us the shadows of the night, and to realize our individuality, and the coming of our Judge. The night is far spent, the day is at hand. "Be sober and watch."

SEES THEM

LET us ever make it our prayer and our endeavour, that we may know the whole counsel of God, and grow unto the measure of the stature of the fulness of Christ; that all prejudice, and self-confidence, and hollowness, and unreality, and positiveness, and partisanship, may be put away from us under the light of Wisdom, and the fire of Faith and Love; till we see things as God sees them, with the judgment of His Spirit, and according to the mind of Christ. Amen.

ON TRIAL

WE ARE all on our trial. Every one who lives is on his trial, whether he will serve God or not. And we read in Scripture of many instances of the trials upon which Almighty God puts us His creatures. In the beginning, Adam, when he was first created, was put on his trial. He was placed in a beautiful garden, he had everything given him for his pleasure and comfort; he was created innocent and upright, and he had the great gift of the Holy Spirit given him to enable him to please God, and to attain heaven. One thing alone he was forbidden—to eat of the tree of the knowledge of good and evil; this was his trial. If he did not eat of the fruit, he was to live; if he did, he was to die. Alas, he did eat of the fruit and he did die. He was tried and found wanting; he fell; such was the end of *his* trial.

How much is there in this melancholy history which applies to us, my brethren, at this day, though it happened some thousand years ago! Man is the same in every age, and God Almighty is the same; and thus what happened to Adam is, alas! daily fulfilled in us, to our great shame.

KINGS

WE ALL have been raised by God to great honour and glory; not, indeed, glory of this world, but unseen spiritual glory. We were born in sin, and the children of wrath; and He has caused us to be baptized with water and the Spirit in the Name of Father, Son, and Holy Ghost; and as Saul, by being anointed with oil by Samuel, was made king of Israel, so we, by baptism, are made kings, not kings of this world, but kings and princes in the heavenly kingdom of Christ.

IN PROSPECT

HE IS our head, and we are His brethren; He has sat down on His throne on high, and has been crowned by His eternal Father as Lord and Christ; and we, too, by being made His brethren, partake His unseen, His heavenly glory. Though we be

poor in this world, yet, when we were baptized we, like Saul, were made strong in
the Lord, powerful princes, with Angels
to wait upon us, and with a place on
Christ's throne in prospect. "Our Father,
who art in heaven, etc."

BEARING TRIAL

HOW MANY are there who, when in distress of any kind, in want of means, or of
necessaries, forget, like Saul, that their distress, whatever it is, comes from God; that
God brings it on them, and that God will
remove it in His own way, if they trust
in Him: but who, instead of waiting for
His time, take their own way, their own
bad way, and impatiently hasten the time,
and thus bring on themselves judgment!
Sometimes, telling an untruth will bring
them out of their difficulties and they are
tempted to do so. They make light of the
sin; they say they cannot help themselves,
that they are forced to it, as Saul said to
Samuel; they make excuses to quiet their
conscience; and instead of bearing their
trial well, enduring their poverty, or whatever the trouble may be, they do not

shrink from a deliberate sin which God hates.

Again, how many are there who, when in unpleasant situations, are tempted to do what is wrong in order to flee them, instead of patiently waiting God's time! When persons have harsh masters and employers, or troublesome neighbors, or are engaged in employments which they do not like, they often forget that all this is from God's providence, that to Him they must look up, that He who imposed it can take it away, can take it away in His good time, and without their sin.

Consider this, my soul, and lay it to heart. Doubtless I must render myself to God's mercy here, or else be forced away from His anger hereafter.

"Today if you shall hear His voice, harden not your hearts."

SECRET GIFT

THOSE who obey God and follow Christ have secret gains, so great, that, as well might we say heaven were like hell, as that these are like the gain which sinners have. They have a secret gift given them by their Lord and Saviour in proportion to their faith and love. They cannot describe it to others; they have not possession of it all at once; they cannot have the enjoyment of it at this or that time when they will. It comes and goes according to the will of the Giver. It is given but in small measure to those who begin God's service. It is not given to those who follow Him with a divided heart.

But those who give themselves up to their Lord and Saviour, those who surrender themselves soul and body, those who honestly say, "I am Thine, new-make me, do with me what Thou wilt," who say so not once or twice merely, or in a transport, but calmly and habitually; these are they who gain the Lord's secret gift, even the "white counter, and in the counter a new name written which no man knoweth, but he that receiveth it."

BEAR FRUIT

TIME is short, eternity is long; I am weak; I stand between heaven and hell; Thou art my Saviour; Thou hast suffered for me; the Holy Ghost sanctifies me; repentance purifies me. Let me receive these truths in reverence, and pray Thee to give me a good will, and divine light, and spiritual strength, that they may bear fruit within me. Amen.

NOT CONSUME

I HAVE an instinct within me which leads me to rise and go to my Father, to name the Name of His well-beloved Son, and having named it, to place myself unreservedly in His hands, saying, "If Thou, O Lord, will mark iniquities, Lord, who shall stand it? For with Thee there is merciful forgiveness." This is the feeling in which I come to confess my sins, and to pray Thee for pardon and grace day by day; and I know it is the very feeling in which I must prepare to meet Thee when Thou comest visibly.

That hour must come at length upon every one of us. When it comes, may the countenance of the Most Holy quicken, not consume me; may the flame of judgment be to me only what it was to the Three Holy Children over whom the fire had no power! Amen.

FOR TOMORROW

WHO would care for any loss or gain to-day, if he knew for certain that Christ would show Himself tomorrow? No one. So too the true Christian feels as he would feel, did he know for certain that Christ would be here tomorrow.

I know for certain that Christ will come to me when I die; and faith antici-pates my death and makes it just as if that distant day, if it *be* distant, were past and over. One time or another, Christ will come, for certain: and when once He *has* come, it matters not what length of time there was before He came:—however long that period may be, it has an end.

Judgment is coming, whether it comes sooner or later, and the Christian realises that it is coming; that is, time should not enter into my calculation, or interfere with my view of things. I shall not be solicitous for tomorrow; for the morrow will be solicitous for itself.

Let me not fear opposition, suspicion, reproach or ridicule. God sees me; and His Angels, they are looking on. Yet a very little while, He that cometh will not delay.

SON OF GOD

THOU it was who didst create the world; Thou it was who didst interpose of old time in the affairs of the world, and showed Thyself to be a living and observant God, whether men thought of Thee or not.

Yet, Thou, great God, didst condescend to come down on earth from Thy heavenly throne, and to be born into Thy own world; showing Thyself as the Son of God in a new and second sense, in a created human nature, as well as in Thy eternal substance.

HE IS COME

MAY it be my blessedness, as years go on, to add one grace to another, and advance upward, step by step, neither neglecting the lower after attaining the higher, nor aiming at the higher before attaining the lower. The first grace is faith, the last is love; first comes zeal, afterwards comes loving-kindness; first comes diligence, then comes resignation.

May I learn to mature all graces in

me; fearing and trembling, watching and repenting, because Christ is coming; joyful, thankful, and careless of the future because He is come. Amen.

NOT REST OR TARRY

WHEN Thou camest into the world, Thou wert a pattern of sanctity in the circumstances of Thy life, as well as in Thy birth. Thou camest down from heaven, and didst make a short work and then didst return back again where Thou wert before. Thou camest into the world, and Thou speedily didst leave the world; as if to teach us how little Thou Thyself, how little we Thy followers, should have to do with the world.

Thou, Eternal Ever-living Word of God, didst not outlive Methuselah's years, nay, did not even exhaust the common age of man; but Thou didst come and Thou didst go, before men knew that Thou had come, like the lightning from one side of heaven unto the other, as being the beginning of a new creation and invisible creation, and having no part in the old Adam.

Thou wert in the world but not of the world; and while Thou wert here, Thou, the Son of man, wert still in heaven: and as well might fire feed upon water, or the wind be subjected to man's bidding, as the Only-begotten Son really be portion and member of that perishable system in which Thou condescendest to move. Thou couldst not rest or tarry upon earth; Thou didst but do Thy work in it; Thou couldst but come and go.

NOT TURN AWAY

I MUST learn to know myself, and to have thoughts and feelings becoming myself. Impetuous hope and undisciplined mirth ill-suit a sinner. Should I shrink from low notions of myself and sharp pain and mortification of natural wishes, whose guilt called down the Son of God from heaven to die upon the Cross for me? May I live in pleasure here, and call this world my home, while I read in the Gospel of my Saviour's life-long affliction and disappointment?

It cannot be; let me prepare for suffering and disappointment, which befit me as a sinner and which are as necessary for me as for saints. Let me not turn away from trial when God brings it on me, or play the coward in the fight of faith. "Watch ye, stand fast in the faith, do manfully, be strengthened"; such is St. Paul's exhortation. When affliction overtakes me, let me remember to accept it as a means of improving my heart, and pray God for His grace that it may be so; that I may look disappointment in the face.

Let my light shine before men, let me praise God by a consistent life, even though others do not seem to glorify their Father on account of it, or to be benefited by my example. Amen.

IN CHRIST JESUS

NOTHING can harm us who bear Christ within us. Trial or temptation, time of tribulation, time of health, pain, bereavement, anxiety, sorrow, nothing can separate us from the love of God, which is in Christ Jesus our Lord.

Things of this world are only valuable so far as God's Presence is in them, so far as He has breathed on them; in themselves they are but dust and vanity; and it is as monstrous and insane, if I thought aright, to be enamoured of anything earthly, except it be instinct with a light from heaven, as to desire to feed on ashes, or to be chained to a corpse.

DAY BY DAY

WE HAVE the history of all the Confessors and Martyrs of early times and since, to show us that Christ's arm is not shortened; that faith and love have a real abiding-place on earth; that, come what will, His grace is sufficient for His Church and His strength made perfect in weakness; that even to old age, and to hoar hairs, He will carry and deliver her; that, in whatever time the powers of evil give challenge, Martyrs and Saints will start forth again, and rise from the dead, as plentiful as though they had never been before. Meantime, let me aim at obeying God, in all things, little as great, day by day, for sufficient for the day is the evil thereof. Amen.

STANDING OVER ME

WHEREVER faith in Christ is, there is Christ Himself. He said to Martha, "believest thou this?" Wherever there is a heart to answer, "Yes, Lord, I have believed," there Christ is present. There our Lord vouchsafes to stand, though unseen, whether over the bed of death or over the grave; whether we ourselves are sinking or those around us. Blessed be Thy Name! Nothing can rob me of this consolation: I will be as certain, through Thy grace, that Thou art standing over me in love, as though I saw Thee. Only, I will beg of Thee a more understanding view of the mystery of Thy Cross. Thou wilt never put upon me more than I can bear, never afflict me with any woe except for my own highest benefit. Amen.

Let me make up my mind to take Thee for my portion, and pray to Thee for grace to enable me so to do. Amen.

One sight of Thy divine countenance, so tender, so loving, so majestic, so calm, was enough, first to convert St. Paul, then, to support him on his way amid the bitter hatred and fury which he was to excite in

those who hitherto had loved him. And
if such be the momentary vision of Thy
glorious presence, what will be my bliss,
to whom it shall be given, this life ended,
to see Thy Face eternally?

THE CRUCIFIED

LET me think of the Cross when I rise
and when I lie down, when I go out and
when I come in, when I eat and when I
walk and when I converse, when I buy
and when I sell, when I labour and when
I rest, consecrating and sealing all my
doings with this one mental action, the
thought of the Crucified. Let me not argue
about it with others; but be silent, like
the penitent Magdalen, who showed her
love in deep subdued acts. She stood at
His feet behind Him weeping, and began
to wash His feet with tears, and wiped
them, with the hairs of her head, and
kissed His feet, and anointed them with
the ointment. And Christ said of her,
"Many sins are forgiven her, because she
hath loved much; but to whom less is
forgiven, he loveth less."

OUR PRAYERS

AND FURTHER, let me dwell often upon those, His manifold mercies to me and to my brethren, which are the consequence of His coming upon earth; His adorable counsels, as manifested in my personal vocation; how it is that I am called and others not; the wonders of His grace towards me, from my infancy until now; the gifts He has given me; the aid He has vouchsafed; the answers He has accorded to my prayers. "O, my God, I love Thee, etc."

PRODIGAL SONS

THERE is a time when the presence of the Most High would at first sight seem to be intolerable: when first the consciousness vividly bursts upon us that we have ungratefully rebelled against Him. Yet so it is that true repentance cannot be without the thought of God; it has the thought of God, for it seeks Him; and it seeks Him, because it is quickened with love; and even sorrow must have a sweetness, if love be in it. For what is it to repent but to surrender ourselves to God for pardon or punishment; as loving His presence for its own sake, and accounting chastisement from Him better than rest and peace from the world?

While the prodigal son remained among the swine, he had sorrow enough, but no repentance; remorse only; but repentance led him to his Father, and to confess his sins. Thus he relieved his heart of its misery, which before was like some hard and fretful tumour weighing upon it. "O my God, I am sorry."

TO REPENTANCE

CONSIDER St. Paul's account of the repentance of the Corinthians; there is sorrow in abundance, nay, anguish, but no gloom, no dryness of spirit, no sternness. The penitents afflict themselves, but it is from the fullness of their hearts, from love, gratitude, devotion, horror of the past, desire to escape from their present selves into some state holier and more heavenly. St. Paul approves of their earnest desire, their mourning, their fervent mind towards him. He rejoices, not that they were made sorry, but that they sorrowed to repentance. "O my God, I hope in Thee, because, etc."

TRUE REFUGE

OFTEN we are pent up within ourselves, and are therefore miserable. Perhaps we may not be able to analyze our misery, or even to realize it, as persons oftentimes who are in bodily sicknesses. We do not know, perhaps, what or where our pain is; we are so used to it that we do not call it pain. Still so it is; we need a relief to our hearts, that they may be dark and sullen no longer, or that they may not go on feeding upon themselves to something beyond; and much as we may wish it otherwise, and may try to make idols to ourselves, nothing short of God's presence is our true refuge; everything else is either a mockery, or but an expedient useful for its season or in its measure. "O my God, I love Thee."

MY PORTION

ARE we allowed to put ourselves upon His guidance? This surely is the only question. Has He really made us His children, and taken possession of us by His Holy Spirit? Are we still in His kingdom of grace, in spite of our sins? The question is not whether we should go, but whether He will receive. And we trust, that, in spite of our sins, He will receive us still, every one of us, if we seek His face in love unfeigned, and holy fear. Let us say with the Psalmist. "What have I in heaven? and besides Thee what do I desire upon earth? My flesh and my heart have fainted away; Thou art the God of my heart . . . my portion forever." Amen.

GIFTS

NO DOUBT the greater number of persons who try to live Christian lives, and who observe themselves with any care, are dissatisfied with their own state on this point, viz., that, whatever their religious strivings may be, yet they feel that their motive is not the highest; that the love of God, and of man for His sake, is not their ruling principle. They may do much, nay, if it so happen, they may suffer much; but they have little reason to think that they love much, that they do and suffer for love's sake.

Not thus do they express themselves exactly, but they are dissatisfied with themselves, and when this dissatisfaction is examined into, it will be found ultimately to come to this, though they will give different accounts of it. They may call themselves cold, or hard-hearted, or fickle, or double-minded or doubting, or dim-sighted, or weak in resolve, but they mean pretty much the same thing, that their affections do not rest on Almighty God as their great Object. Thus will be found the complaint of religious men among ourselves, not less than others; their reason and their heart not going together; their reason tending heavenwards, and their heart earthwards. Yet St. Paul emphatically assures us that his acceptance with God did not stand in any of those high endowments, which strike us in him, at first sight, and which, did we actually see

St. Paul, doubtless would so much draw us to him.

One of St. Paul's highest gifts was his spiritual knowledge. He shared and felt the sinfulness and infirmities of human nature; he had a deep insight into the glories of God's grace, such as no natural man can have. He had an awful sense of the realities of heaven, and of the mysteries revealed. He could have answered ten thousand questions on theological subjects, on all those points about which theologians disputed since his time, and which we so long to ask him. He was a man whom one could not come near, without going away from him wiser than one came; a fount of knowledge and wisdom ever full, ever approachable, ever flowing, from which all who came in full gained a measure of the gifts which God had lodged in him.

PRACTICING CHARITY

HIS presence inspired resolutions, confidence, and zeal, as one who was the keeper of secrets, and the revealer of the whole counsel of God; and who, by look and word and deed encompassed, as it were, his brethren with God's mercies and judgments; spread abroad and reared aloft the divine system of doctrine and precept, and seated himself and them securely in the midst of it. Such was this great servant of Christ and Teacher of the Gentiles; yet he says, "If I speak with the tongues of men, and of angels, if I should have prophecy and should know all mysteries, and all knowledge, and have not charity, I am become as sounding brass, or a tinkling cymbal . . . I am nothing."

Clearly then we must practice love. He who loves cares little for anything else. The world may go as it will; he sees and hears it not, for his thoughts are drawn another way; he is solicitous mainly to walk with God, and to be found with God; and is in perfect peace because he is stayed in Him. Till we, in a certain sense, detach ourselves from our bodies, our minds will not be in a state to receive divine impressions, and to exert heavenly aspirations.

A smooth and easy life, an uninterrupted enjoyment of the goods of Providence, full meals, soft raiment, well furnished homes, the pleasure of sense, the feeling of security, the consciousness of wealth, these and the like, if we are not careful, choke up all the avenues of the soul, through which the light and breath of heaven might come to us. We must, at least at seasons, defraud ourselves of nature, if we would not be defrauded of grace, we must do penance by practicing charity. St. Paul, pray for us.

TEMPLES OF CHRIST

THEN we do everything thankfully and joyfully, when we are temples of Christ, with His Image set up in us. Then it is that we mix with the world without loving it, for our affections are given to another. We can bear to look on the world's beauty, for we have no heart for it. We are not disturbed at its frowns, for we live not in its smiles.

I have lost friends, I have lost the world, but I have gained Him, who gives in Himself houses and brethren and sisters and mothers and children and lands a hundred-fold; I have lost the perishable, and gained the Infinite; I have lost time, and I have gained eternity.

RAYS OF LOVE

OH MAY we be loyal and affectionate before our race is run! Before our sun goes down in the grave, oh may we learn somewhat more of what the Apostle calls the love of Christ which passeth knowledge, and catch some of the rays of love which come from Him! Especially at the season of the year now approaching, when Christ calls us in the wilderness, let us gird up our loins and fearlessly obey the summons. Let us take up our cross and follow him. Let us take to us "the whole armor of God, that we may be able to stand against the wiles of the devil; for we wrestle not against flesh and blood, but against principalities, against powers, against the rulers of the darkness of the world, against spiritual wickedness in high places; wherefore, take unto you the whole armor of God, that ye may be able to withstand in the evil day, and having done all, to stand."

In the Catholic Church it is the one Virgin Mother, one and the same from first to last, and Catholics have ever acknowledged her. May not our devotion to her be scanty. May it be overflowing.

WORDS OF GOD

IN VAIN does the whole Psalter, from beginning to end, proclaim and protest that the world is against the truth, and that the saints must suffer. In vain do Apostles proclaim that the world lieth in wickedness; in vain does Christ Himself declare, that broad is the way that leadeth to destruction, and many there be that go in thereat. In vain do Prophets foretell that in the end the saints shall possess the kingdom,—implying they do not possess it now. In vain is the vast judgment of the Deluge; in vain the instant Death of the first-born in Egypt, and of the hosts of Sennacherib. No, men will not believe; the words of the Tempter ring in their ears,—"You shall not die!" and men stake their eternal interests on sight and reason, rather than on the revealed Word of God.

GOD AND JUDGE

OH HOW miserable in that day, when the dead bones rise from their graves, and the millions who once lived are summoned before their Omnipotent Judge, whose breath is a fiery stream, and whose voice is like the sound of many waters! How vain to call upon the rocks to fall on us; or to attempt to hide ourselves among the trees of the garden, and to make our brother's sin cover our own; when we are in His presence, who is everywhere at once, and is as fully and entirely our God and Judge, as if there were no other creature but each of us in the whole world!

TO PLEASE GOD

LET me leave the world, manifold and various as it is; let me leave it to follow its own devices, and let me turn to the living and true God, who has revealed Himself to me in Jesus Christ. Let me be sure that He is more true than the whole world, though with one voice all its inhabitants were to speak against Him.

Let me pray Him to give me humility, that I may seek aright; honesty, that I may have no concealed aims; love, that I may desire the truth; and faith, that I may accept it. So that when the end comes, and the multitudes who have joined hands in evil are punished, I may be of those who are "delivered." Let me put off all excuses, all unfairness and insincerity, all trifling with my conscience, all self-deception, all delay of repentance. Let me be filled with one wish,—to please God; and if I have this, I say it confidently, I shall no longer be deceived by this world, however loud it speaks, and however plausibly it argues, as if God were with it, for I shall "have an unction from the Holy One," and shall "know all things." Amen.

A THANKFUL SPIRIT

"IN ALL things give thanks; for this is the will of God in Christ Jesus concerning you all." St. Paul, who writes thus, was himself an especial pattern of a thankful spirit: "Rejoice in the Lord always; again I say, rejoice." "I have learned in whatever state I am to be content therewith." "I can do all things in Him who strengthened me."

"I obtained the mercy of God, because I did it ignorantly in unbelief."

MY SAVIOUR

WHAT is it to me how my future path lies, if it be but Thy path? Whither it leads, so that in the end it leads to Thee? What terror befalls me if Thou be but at hand to protect and strengthen me? Thou art my Lord God, the Holy One of Israel, my Saviour. Amen.

Thou art the Way, the Truth, the Life. Thou art a light unto my ways and a lanthorn unto my paths. Thou art my Shepherd. May I know Thy voice. Let me beware of receiving Thy grace in vain. Let me look out for Thee who alone can guide me. I am safe while I keep close to Thee and under Thy eye. Amen.

STAND FAST

THE DEATH and resurrection of Christ is ever a call upon me to die to time, and to live to eternity. Let me not be satisfied with the state in which I find myself; let me not be satisfied with nature; let me be satisfied with grace. Let me beware of taking up with a low standard of duty, and aiming at nothing but what I can easily fulfill. Let me pray God to enlighten me with a knowledge of the extent of my duty, to enlighten me with a true view of this world. Let me beware lest the world seduce me. It will aim at persuading me that it is rational and sensible, that religion is very well in its way, but that I am born to enjoy the world. And I shall be seduced most certainly, unless I watch and pray that I enter not into temptation. I must either conquer the world, or the world will conquer me. I must be either master or slave. Let me take my part then, and "stand fast—by the freedom wherewith Christ has made us free." Amen.

THE GIVER

ST. PAUL was smitten immediately. Suddenly and utterly does our strength, and our holiness, and our blessedness, and our influence, depart from us, like a lamp that expires, or a weight that falls, as soon as we rest in them, and pride ourselves in them, instead of referring them to the Giver. God keep us in His mercy from this sin! St. Paul shows us how we should feel about God's gifts, and how to boast without pride, when he first says, "I laboured more abundantly than all they"; and then adds "yet not I, but the grace of God with me."

Accordingly, the self-respect of the Christian is no personal and selfish feeling, but rather a principle of loyal devotion and reverence towards that Divine Master who condescends to visit him. He acts, not hastily, but under restraint and fearfully, as understanding that God's eye is over him, and God's hand upon him, and God's voice within him. He acts with the recollection that his Omniscient Guide is also his future Judge; and that while He moves him, He is also noting down in His book how he answers to His godly motions. He acts with a memory laden with past infirmity and sin; and a consciousness that he has much more to mourn over and repent of, in the years gone by, than to rejoice in. Yes, surely, he has many a secret wound to be healed; many a bruise to be tended; many a sore, like Lazarus; many a chronic infirmity; many a bad omen of perils to come. It is one thing, not to trust in the world; it is another thing to trust in one's self.

WITHOUT GLOOM

LET me rejoice then while I mourn. Let me look up to my Lord and Saviour the more I shrink from the sight of myself; let me have the more faith and love, the more I exercise repentance.

All the beauty of nature, the kind influence of the seasons, the gifts of sun and moon, and the fruits of the earth, the advantages of civilized life, and the presence of friends and intimates; all these good things are but one extended and wonderful type of God's benefits in the Gospel.

Those who aim at perfection will not reject the gift, but add a corrective; they will add the bitter herbs to the fatted calf and the music and dancing; they will not refuse the flowers of earth, but they will toil in plucking up the weeds, or if they refrain from the temporal blessing, it will be to reserve another; for this is one great mercy of God, that while He allows us a discretionary use of His temporal gifts, He allows a discretionary abstinence also; and He almost enjoins upon us the use of some, lest we should forget that this earth is His creation, and not of the evil one.

May God give me grace to walk thus humbly, thus soberly, thus without censoriousness in this day of confusion; enjoying His blessings, yet taking them with fear and trembling; and disciplining myself without gloom. Amen.

HIS EARTHLY NAME

WHAT high things are told us in the New Testament concerning the Name of Jesus, what reverence towards it is enjoined us, and what virtue is ascribed to it! The earthly Name of the Son of God—that Name which is to be above every name, at which every knee is to bow, of things in heaven, and things in earth, and things under the earth; that Name which cast out devils, restored the crippled, and did many wonderful works; that Name, which is like ointment poured out, and which shall endure forever among the posterities—how should not some large bountifulness in act accompany such grace in words?

YET SINNERS

CHRIST has done the whole work of redemption for us; and yet it is no contradiction to say, that something remains for us to do. We have to take the redemption offered us, and that taking involves a work. We have to apply His grace to our own souls, and that application implies pain, trial, and toil, in the midst of its blessedness. He has suffered and conquered, and those who become partakers in Him undergo in their own persons the shadow and likeness of that passion and victory. In them, one by one, is acted over again and again the history of the Son of God, so that as He died they die to sin, as He rose again, so they rise again to righteousness; and in this imitation of His history consists their participation of His glory. He truly has planted us in the land of promise, and has given our enemies into our hands; but they are still in it, and they have to be expelled from it.

The word "Jesus" means the Saviour; it has reference then to sinners. He came not to call the just but sinners to repentance. "For scarcely will any one die on behalf of a just man; but while we were yet sinners, Christ died in our behalf." Glory be to the Father, the Son and the Holy Ghost.

OF GOD

WHEN Christ came, he inherited the earth by the right of His heavenly Father, and by no earthly pretension. He came not as the emperor of the world, or as a claimant of any earthly throne; nor was He of the priestly line; but "without father, without mother, without genealogy," as far as any temporal prerogative flowed from it; born miraculously; prospered miraculously; "not of blood, nor of the will of the flesh, nor of the will of man, but of God."

THY OWN TIME

MAY I henceforth be more diligent than heretofore in keeping the mirror of my heart unsullied and bright, so as to reflect the image of the Son of God in the Father's presence, clean from the dust and stains of the world, from envies and jealousies, strife and debate, bitterness and harshness, indolence and impurity, care and discontent, deceit and meanness, arrogance and boasting!

What were Thy thoughts, if I may venture to use such language or to admit such a reflection concerning the Infinite, when human feelings, human sorrows, human wants, first become Thine? What a mystery is there from first to last in Thy becoming man! Yet in proportion to the mystery is the grace and mercy of it; and as is the grace, so is the greatness of the fruit of it.

Keep my mind from running to waste; calm, soothe, sober, steady it; attune it to Thy will, teach it to love all men, to be cheerful and thankful, and to be resigned in all the dispensations of Thy providence towards me. Good Lord, fulfill Thy purpose towards me in Thy own time! Amen.

ZEAL

LOVE or Charity as described by St. Paul is not merely brotherly-love, but a general temper of gentleness, meekness, sympathy, tender consideration, open-heartedness towards all men, brother or stranger, who come in our way. Thus the Saints of God go on unto perfection. Moses ended his life as "the meekest of men," though he began it with undisciplined zeal, which led him to a deed of violence. St. John, who would call down fire from heaven, became the Apostle of Love; St. Paul, who persecuted Christ's servants, was made all things to all men; yet neither of them lost his zeal, though they trained it to be spiritual. May Almighty God, for His dear Son's sake, lead us safely through these dangerous times, so that we may never lose our zeal for His honor but may sanctify it by Faith and Charity, neither staining our garments by wrath or violence, nor soiling them with the dust of a turbulent world. Amen.

TRUTH TO OTHERS

THE DANGER of education is that it separates feeling and acting; it teaches us to think, speak, and be affected aright, without forcing us to practice what is right. St. Luke and St. Paul show us that we may be sturdy workers in the Lord's service and bear our cross manfully, though we be adorned with all learning; that the graces of a cultivated mind may be a means of introducing and recommending the Truth to others. Let us then apply St. Paul's precept to preach the word in season, out of season; reprove, entreat, rebuke, in all patience.

PREPARATION

THIS WORLD is to be a world of practice and labor; God reveals to us glimpses of the Third Heaven for our comfort. The Sacrifice of the Mass, day by day, obedience to God in our calling and in ordinary matters, endeavors to imitate our Saviour Christ in word and deed, constant prayer to Him, may these be our due preparation for receiving and profiting by His revelations. Amen.

ALSO ON EARTH

THAT we may understand that in spite of Thy mysterious perfections Thou hast a separate knowledge and regard for me individually, Thou hast taken upon Thyself the thoughts and feelings of my own nature, which I know is capable of personal attachment. Thou art not simply an unchangeable Creator to rely upon, but a compassionate Guardian, a discriminating Judge and Helper.

Thou didst altogether dishonor what the world esteems, when Thou didst take on Thyself a rank and station which the world despises. Thou dost teach me to be cheerful and joyful in the midst of those obscure and ordinary circumstances of life which the world passes over and thinks scorn of.

I do not realize the wonderful truth that Thou dost see and think of me individually; that Thou art really present everywhere, that Thou art wherever I am, though unseen; that Thou seest what is going on among ourselves at this moment; that this man falls and that man is exalted, at Thy silent, invisible appointment. May I know that Thou who art in heaven forgetteth not that Thou art also on earth. Amen.

VERY AND ETERNAL

ALL the time Jesus was on earth, when He was conceived, when He was born, when He was tempted, on the Cross, in the grave, and now at God's right hand,—all the time through, He was the Eternal and Unchangeable Word, the Son of God. The Apostles, Disciples, Priests and Pharisees, and the multitude, all who saw Thee in the flesh, my Jesus, saw, as the whole earth and I shall see Thee at the last day, the Very and Eternal Son of God.

TO JUDGE

THOU didst have a man's heart, a man's tears, and a man's wants and infirmities. From the time Thou wast born of the Virgin Mary, Thou didst have a natural fear of danger, a natural shrinking from pain. Give me a heart and understanding to realize that Thou, the Only-begotten Son, our Lord, didst suffer, arise from the dead, ascend into heaven, whence Thou shalt come again, at the end of the world to judge the quick and the dead! Amen.

LITTLE ONES

GOD grant to me a simple, reverent, affectionate mind, the mind of those little ones, whose Angels always see the face of our Father. This gained, the rest through Thy grace will follow. Amen.

THY SAKE

MAY I rejoice in Thee and in all Thy Creatures see Thee. May I enjoy Thy temporal bounty and partake the pleasant things of earth with Thee in my thoughts; may I rejoice in my friends for Thy sake, loving them most especially because Thou hast loved them. Amen.

THY GRACE

MAY I labor, not in my own strength, but in the power of God the Holy Spirit, to be sober, chaste, temperate, meek, affectionate, good, faithful, firm, humble, patient, cheerful, resigned, under all circumstances, at all times, among all people, amid all trials and sorrows of this mortal life! May God grant me the grace, according to His promise, through His Son our Saviour Jesus Christ! Amen.

HEAVENLY PORTION

MAY God give me grace so to hear what has been said, as I shall wish to have heard, when life is over; to hear in a practical way, with a desire to profit by it, to learn God's will, and to do it!

Thou art All-merciful, though All-righteous; and though Thou art awful in Thy judgments, Thou art nevertheless more wonderfully pitiful and of tender compassion above our largest expectations, and in the case of all who humbly seek Thee, Thou wilt in wrath remember mercy. Amen.

May Thou grant Thy grace abundantly to me to make me meet for Thy presence that I may not be ashamed before Thee at Thy coming! May Thou vouchsafe to me the full grace of Thy sacraments: may Thou feed me with Thy choicest gift: may Thou expel the poison from my soul: may Thou wash me clean in Thy precious Body and Blood, and give me the fullness of faith, love and hope, as foretastes of the heavenly portion which Thou destinest for me. Amen.

THE FEAST

ALL that our Saviour has done is again and again shadowed out in the Old Testament: His miraculous birth, His life, His teachings, His death, His priesthood, His sacrifice, His resurrection, His glorifications, His kingdom, are again and again prefigured. It is not reasonable to suppose that the great gift should be omitted. He who died for us, is He who feeds us; and as His death is mentioned, so we may beforehand expect will be mentioned the feast He gives us.

The great gift was shadowed out in the description of the promised land, which was said to flow with milk and honey, and in all those other precious things of nature which are recounted as belonging to the promised land, oil, butter, corn, wine, and the like. These were all destined to refer to the Gospel feast typically, because they were the rarest and most exquisite of the blessings given to the Jews, as the Gospel Feast is the most choice and the most sacred and most precious of all the blessings given to us Catholics.

FIRST FRUITS

SO LET me come to Thee in faith and hope, and let me say to myself, may this be the beginning to me of everlasting bliss! May Thy Body and Thy Blood be the first-fruits of that Banquet which is to last for ever and ever; ever new, ever transporting, inexhaustible, in the city of my God! Amen.

OUR CONVERSATION

ST. PAUL says, "our conversation is in heaven," or in other words, heaven is our city. We know what it is to be a citizen of this world; it is to have interests, rights, privileges, duties, connections, in some particular town or state; to depend upon it, and to be bound to defend it; to be part of it. Now all this the Christian is in respect to heaven. Heaven is his city, earth is not. So it was as regards the Christians of Scripture. As the same Apostle says in another place, we have not here a lasting city, but we seek that which is to come.

AS WE FORGIVE

OUR LORD gives us a pattern in His Prayer, in which we ask that our trespasses may be forgiven, *as* we forgive those who trespass against us; words which are quite out of place, or rather words which will do us harm, if we are not what Christians should be in spirit, but remember injuries and cherish malice. ". . . as we forgive those . . ."

FATHER FORGIVE THEM

OUR LORD had laid aside His glory, He had (as it were) disbanded His legions of Angels, He came on earth without arms, except the arms of truth, meekness, and righteousness, and committed Himself to the world in perfect innocence and sinlessness, and in utter helplessness, as the Lamb of God. For our example, He prayed, "Father, forgive them."

INHERITORS

ALAS, that while we grow in knowledge in matters of time and sense, yet we remain children in knowledge of our heavenly privileges! St. Paul says that whereas Christ is risen, He hath raised us up together, and made us sit together in the heavenly places in Christ Jesus. This is what we have still to learn; to know our place, position, situation as children of God, members of Christ, and inheritors of the kingdom of heaven.

THE SUBSTANCE

WE ARE risen again, and we know it not. We begin our Catechism by confessing that we are risen, but it takes a long life to apprehend what we confess. We are like people waking from sleep, who cannot collect their thoughts at once, or understand where they are. By little and little the truth breaks upon us. Such are we in the present world: sons of light, gradually waking to a knowledge of themselves. For this let us meditate, let us pray, let us work, gradually to attain to a real apprehension of what we are. Thus, as time goes on, we shall gain first one thing, then another. By little and little we shall give up shadows and find the substance.

UNDERSTANDING

WAITING on God day by day, we shall make progress day by day, and approach to the true and clear view of what He has made us to be in Christ. Year by year we shall gain something and each Easter, as it comes, will enable us more to rejoice with heart and understanding in that great salvation which Christ then accomplished.

MORE DEVOTED

THIS we shall find to be one great providential benefit arising from those duties which He exacts of us. Our duties to God and man are not only duties done to Him, but they are means of enlightening our eyes and making our faith apprehensive. Every act of religion has a tendency to strengthen our convictions about heaven. Every sacrifice makes us more zealous; every self-denial makes us more devoted.

This is a use, too, of the observance of sacred seasons; they wean us from this world, they impress upon us the reality of the world which we see not. We trust, if we thus proceed, we shall understand more and more what we are. We humbly trust that, as we cleanse ourselves from this world, our eyes will be enlightened to see the things which are only spiritually discerned. We hope that to us will be fulfilled in due measure the words of the beatitude, "Blessed are the clean of heart, for they shall see God."

DAY-STAR

WE HAVE good hope, which cannot deceive us, that if we wait upon God, as the Saints have ever waited, with fastings and prayers, if we seek Him as Anna sought Him, or St. Peter at Joppa, or holy Daniel before them, Christ will be manifested to us; the day will dawn, and the day-star arise in our hearts.

Our Father, who art in heaven. . , Thy kingdom come. . .

THAT SECRET

WE SHALL see the sign of the Son of man in heaven; we shall eat of the hidden manna, and possess that secret of the Lord which is with those that fear Him; and like St. Paul, we shall know whom we have believed, and are certain that He is able to keep that which we have committed unto Him against that day.

IT ABIDES

WE KNOW, too, that it is the peculiarity of the warfare between the Church and the world, that the world seems ever gaining on the Church, yet the Church is really ever gaining on the world. Its enemies are ever triumphing over it as vanquished, and its members ever discouraged; yet it abides. It abides, and it sees the ruin of its oppressors and enemies. "O how suddenly do they consume, perish, and come to a fearful end!" Kingdoms rise and fall; nations expand and contract; dynasties begin and end; princes are born and die; confederacies are made and unmade, and parties, and companies, and crafts, and guilds, and establishments, and philosophies, and sects and heresies.

THE FUTURE

THEY have their day, but the Church is eternal; yet *in* their day they seem of much account. How in early times must the Church have been dismayed, when, from the East, the false religion of Mahomet spread far and near, and Christians were extirpated or converted to it by thousands! Yet even that long-lived delusion is now failing; and though younger than the Church by some centuries, has aged before it. And so in like manner, in spite of the duration of the Christian name hitherto, much there is to try our faith at this moment, who cannot see the future, and therefore cannot see the short duration of what shows proudly and successfully now. "Our Father, who art in Heaven, hallowed be Thy Name. Thy Kingdom come. Thy will be done on earth as it is in heaven."

SUFFERING

HERE is a fresh mystery in the history of His humiliation, and the thought of it will cast a new and solemn light on the chapters we shall read during Holy Week. I have said that, after His incarnation, man's nature was as much and truly Christ's as His Divine attributes; St. Paul even speaks of God "redeeming us through His own blood," and of the "Lord of Glory" being "killed,"—and expressions which, more than any other, show how absolutely and simply He had put on Him the nature of man. As the soul acts through the body as its instrument, in a more perfect way, but as intimately, did the Eternal Word of God act through the manhood which He had taken. When He spoke, it was literally God speaking; when He suffered, it was God suffering.

PERSONALLY HIS

NOT that the Divine Nature itself could suffer, any more than our soul can see or hear; but, as the soul sees and hears through the organs of the body, so God the Son suffered in that human nature which He had taken to Himself and made His own. And in that nature He did truly suffer; as truly as He framed the worlds through His Almighty power, so through His human nature did He suffer; for when He came on earth, His manhood became as truly and personally His, as His Almighty power had been from everlasting. "I believe in God, the Father Almighty, Creator of Heaven and earth, and in Jesus Christ His only Son, Our Lord, Who was conceived by the Holy Ghost, born of the Virgin Mary, suffered under Pontius Pilate, was crucified, died and was buried."

THE SUFFERER

NOW I bid you consider that that Face, so ruthlessly smitten, was the Face of God Himself; the Brows bloody with the thorns, the sacred Body exposed to view and lacerated with the scourge, the Hands nailed to the Cross, and, afterwards, the Side pierced with the spear; it was the Blood, and the Sacred Flesh, and the Hands, and the Temples, and the Side, and the Feet of God Himself, which the frenzied multitude then gazed upon.

This is so fearful a thought, that when the mind first masters it, surely it will be difficult to think of anything else; so that, while we think of it, we must pray God to temper it to us, and to give us strength to think of it rightly, lest it be too much for us.

Taking into account, then, that Almighty God Himself, God the Son, was the Sufferer, we shall understand better than we have hitherto the description given of Him by the Evangelists; we shall see the meaning of His general demeanor, His silence, and the words He used when He spoke, and Pilate's awe at Him.

REMEMBER THEE

IMAGINE you see Jesus Christ on the Cross, and say to Him with the penitent thief, "Lord, remember me when Thou shalt come into Thy kingdom"; that is, "Remember me Lord, in mercy, remember not my sins, but Thine own cross; remember Thine own sufferings, remember that Thou sufferedst for me, a sinner; remember in the last day that I, during my lifetime, felt Thy sufferings, that I suffered on my cross by Thy side. Remember me then, and make me remember Thee now." Amen.

REJOICE

O LET not your foot slip; or your eye be false, or your ear dull, or your attention flagging! Be not dispirited; be not afraid; keep a good heart; be bold; draw not back;—you will be carried through. Whatever troubles come on you, of mind, body, or estate; from within or from without; from chance or from intent; from friends or foes;—whatever your trouble be, though you be lonely, O children of a heavenly Father, be not afraid! Quit you like men in your day; and when it is over, Christ will receive you to Himself, and your heart shall rejoice, and your joy no man taketh from you.

Glory be to the Father, to the Son, to the Holy Ghost.

TRANQUILLITY

CHRIST is already in that place of peace, which is all in all. He is on the right hand of God. He is hidden in the brightness of the radiance which issues from the everlasting Throne. He is in the very abyss of peace, where there is no voice of tumult or distress, but a deep stillness,—stillness, that greatest and most awful of all goods which we can fancy,—that most perfect of joys, the utter, profound, ineffable tranquillity of the Divine Essence. He has entered into His rest.

REST

O HOW great a good will it be, if, when this troublesome life is over, we in our turn also enter into that same rest,—if the time shall one day come, when we shall enter into His tabernacle above, and hide ourselves under the shadow of His wings; if we shall be in the number of those blessed dead who die in the Lord, and rest from this labor.

UNSEEN WORLD

HERE we are tossing upon the sea, and the wind is contrary. All through the day we are tried and tempted in various ways. We cannot think, speak, or act, but infirmity and sin are at hand. But in the unseen world, where Christ has entered, all is peace.

GREAT MULTITUDE

THERE is the eternal Throne, and a rainbow round about it, like unto an emerald; and in the midst of the throne the Lamb that has been slain, and has redeemed many people by His blood; and round about the throne four and twenty seats for as many elders, all clothed in white raiment, and crowns of gold upon their heads. And four living beings full of eyes before and behind. And seven Angels standing before God, and doing His pleasure unto the ends of the earth. And the Seraphim above. And withal, a great multitude which no man can number, of all nations, and kindreds, and people, and tongues clothed with white robes, and palms in their hands.

GOD'S COUNTENANCE

"DEATH shall be no more, nor mourning, nor crying, nor sorrow shall be any more; for the former things are passed away." Nor any more sin; nor any more guilt; nor more remorse; no more punishment; no more penitence; no more trial; no infirmity to depress us; no affection to mislead us; no passion to transport us; no prejudice to blind us; no sloth, no pride, no envy, no strife; but the light of God's countenance, and a pure river of water of life, clear as crystal, proceeding out of the throne.

OUR COMING

THAT is our home; here we are but on pilgrimage, and Christ is calling us home. He calls us to His many mansions, which He has prepared. And the Spirit and the Bride call us too, and all things will be ready for us by the time of our coming. "Seeing then that we have a great High Priest that has passed into the heavens, Jesus the Son of God, let us hold fast our confession," seeing we have "so great a

cloud of witnesses, let us lay aside every
weight"; "let us labor to enter into our
rest"; "let us come with confidence unto
the Throne of grace," that we may obtain
mercy, and find grace to help in seasonable aid. Amen.

ATTAIN

IN HEAVEN is the substance, of which
here below we are vouchsafed the image;
and thither, if we be worthy, we shall at
length attain. There is the holy Jerusalem,
whose light is like unto a stone most precious, even like a jasper stone, clear as crystal; and whose wall is great and high, with
twelve gates, and an Angel at each; whose
glory is the Lord God Almighty, and the
Lamb is the lamp thereof. Amen.

PENTECOST

HE WHO is Omnipresent and Omniscient, touched many hearts at once in many
places; they forthwith, one and all, spoke
one language, not learning it one from the
other, but taught by Him the Song of the
Lamb; or if in one sense by man's teach-

ing too, yet catching and mastering it supernaturally, almost before the words were spoken. Men broke out all at once in His praises, in the east and in the west, in the north and in the south; and the perplexed world searched about in vain whence came that concord of sweet and holy sounds. Upon the first voice of the preacher, upon a hint, upon a mere whisper, in the air, a deep response came from many lips, a deep, full, and ready harmony of many voices, one and all proclaiming Christ. For the Spirit of the Lord had descended and filled the earth; and there were thrilling hearts, and tremulous pulses, and eager eyes in every place.

It was a time of visitation, when the weak became strong, and the last became first. It was the triumph of faith, which saith not, "Who shall ascend into heaven? . . . or, Who shall descend into the deep? but what saith the Scripture? The word is nigh thee, even in Thy mouth and in Thy heart; this is the word of faith which we preach."

For God had come down among them, and was everywhere; the Lord of Angels was walking the earth; He was diffusing

His Presence, and multiplying His Image; and in this sense, as well as that in which He spoke the words, "a man's enemies shall be of his own household." The despised, the hated influence insinuated itself everywhere; the leaven spread, and none could stay it; and in the most unfavorable places, in the family of the haughty senator and fierce soldier, amid the superstitions of idolatry, and the debasement of slavery, the noblest and ablest and the fairest, as well as the brutish and the ignorant, one and all, by a secret charm, became the prey of the Church, and the bondsmen of Christ. And thus a great and widespreading kingdom came into existence all at once, like spring after winter, from within.

OUR REFUGE

THOUGH Joshuah in the Old Testament is a figure of Christ and His followers in that he is a combatant and a conqueror, in one point of view he plainly differs from them. He was bidden use carnal weapons in his warfare; but of ours St. Paul says, "the weapons of our warfare are not carnal, but mighty to God unto the pulling down of fortifications." The armies which follow Christ are "on white horses, clothed in fine linen, white and clean"; and "fine linen are the justifications of saints." Such is the rule of our warfare. We advance by yielding; we rise by falling; we conquer by suffering; we persuade by silence; we become rich by bountifulness; we inherit the earth through meekness; we gain comfort through mourning; we earn glory by penitence and prayer. Heaven and earth shall sooner fall than this rule be reversed; it is the law of Christ's kingdom, and nothing can reverse it but sin. As Acham could cause the defeat of the armies of Israel, so sin, indeed, of whatever kind, habitual, or hidden, or scandalous, may disturb this divine provision, but nothing else.

Let us pray that we may all of us be kept pure from sin; let us pray that at last, when we are well stricken with years, we may be as Joseph, not gifted with riches of this world, or with the blessings of life, or with "the precious things brought forth by the sun" or "the precious things put forth by the moon," but with "a name better than of sons and of daughters and Israelites," "the Eternal God for our refuge, and underneath the everlasting arms."

ST. PETER

"BUT sanctify the Lord Christ in your hearts, being ready always to satisfy every one that asketh you a reason of that hope which is in you. But with modesty and fear." St. Peter's faith was one of his characteristic graces. It was ardent, keen, watchful, and prompt. It dispensed with argument, calculation, deliberation, and delay, whenever it heard the voice of its Lord and Saviour; and it heard that voice even when its accents were low, or when it was unaided by the testimony of the other senses. When Christ appeared walking on the sea, and said, "It is I," Peter answered Him, and said, "Lord, if it be Thou, bid me come to Thee upon the waters." When Christ asked His disciples who He was, Simon Peter answered, "Thou art Christ, the Son of the Living God," and obtained our Lord's blessing for such clear and ready faith.

THE CHRIST

AT ANOTHER time, when Christ asked the Twelve whether they would leave Him as others did, St. Peter said, "Lord to whom shall we go? Thou hast the words of Eternal Life. And we have believed and have known that Thou art the Christ, the Son of God."

After the Resurrection, when he heard from St. John that it was Christ who stood on the shore, he sprang out of the boat in which he was fishing, and cast himself into the sea, in his impatience to come near Him.

Other instances of his faith might be mentioned. If ever faith forgot self, and was occupied with its Great Object, it was the faith of Peter. If in any one, Faith appears in contrast with what we commonly understand by Reason, and with Evidence, it so appears in the instance of Peter. When he reasoned, it was at times when Faith was weak. "When he saw the wind boisterous, he was afraid"; and Christ in consequence called him, "O thou of little faith."

When He had asked, "Who is it that

touched Me?", Peter and others reasoned. "Master," said they, "the multitudes throng and press Thee, and dost Thou say 'Who touched Me?'" And in like manner, when Christ said that he should one day follow Him in the way of suffering, Peter said unto Him, "Why cannot I follow Thee now?"

In the Epistle for St. Peter's feast we have an account of St. Peter, when awakened by the Angel, obeying him implicitly, yet not understanding, while he obeyed. He girt himself, and bound on his sandals, and cast his garment about him, and going out, he followed him, and he knew not that it was true which was done by the angel: but thought he saw a vision. Afterwards, coming to himself, he said, "Now I know in very deed that the Lord hath sent His angel, and hath delivered me."

May we be in the number of those who, with the Blessed Apostle whom we this day commemorate, employ all the powers of their minds to the service of their Lord and Saviour, who are drawn heavenward by His wonder-working grace, whose hearts are filled with His love, who reason in His fear, who seek Him in the way of His commandments, and who thereby believe in Him to the saving of their souls! St. Peter, pray for us.

ST. PAUL'S CROWN

DAVID'S affection was given to a single heart; but there is another spoken of in Scripture, who had a thousand friends and loved each as his own soul, and seemed to live a thousand lives in them; and died a thousand deaths when he must quit them; that great Apostle, whose very heart was broken when his brethren wept; who lived if they stood fast "in the Lord"; who was glad when he was weak and they were strong; and who was willing to have imparted unto them his own soul, because they were "most dear" to him. Yet we read of his bidding farewell to whole Churches, never to see them again. At one time, to the littlest ones of the flock; "and the days being expired," says the Evangelist, "departing we went forward, they all bringing us . . . with their wives and children, till we were out of the city: and we kneeled down on the shore and we prayed. And when we had bid one another farewell, we took ship, and they returned home." At another time, to the rulers of the Church: "And now behold," he says to them, "I know that all you, among whom I have gone preaching the kingdom of God, shall see my face no more. Wherefore, I take you to witness this day, that I am clear from the blood of all men; for I have not spared to declare unto you all the counsel of God. . . . I have not coveted any man's silver, gold, or apparel, . . . I have shewed you all things, how that so laboring you ought to support the weak, and to remember the word of the Lord Jesus, how he said: It is a more blessed thing to give than to receive." And then, when he had finished, "kneeling down, he prayed with them all." And they all wept and fell on Paul's neck, "they kissed him, being grieved most of all for the word which he had said, that they should see his face no more. And they brought him on his way to the ship." There was another time, when he took leave of his "own son in the faith," Timothy, in words more calm, and still more impressive, when his end was nigh: "I am even now ready to be sacri-

ficed," he says, "and the time of my disso-
lution is at hand. I have fought a good
fight, I have finished my course, I have
kept the faith. As to the rest, there is laid
up for me a crown of justice, which the
Lord, the Just Judge, will render to me in
that day." St. Paul, pray for us.

A WARNING

AND what are Jacob, Elias, David, but
memorials and tokens of the Son of Man,
when His work and His labour were coming to an end? Like Jacob, like Ishmael,
like Elias, like St. Matthew. He kept feast
before His departure; and, like David, He
was persecuted by the rulers in Israel;
and, like Naomi, He was deserted by His
friends; and like Ishmael, He cried out,
"I thirst" in a barren and dry land; and
at length, like Jacob, He went to sleep
with a stone for His pillow, in the evening.
And, like St. Paul, He had finished the
work which God gave Him to do, and had
confessed a good confession; and, beyond
St. Paul, "the Prince of this world had
come, and in Him had not any thing."
"He was in the world, and the world was

made by Him, and the world knew Him not. He came unto His own, and His own received Him not." Heavily did He leave, tenderly did He mourn over the country and city which rejected Him. "When He drew near, seeing the city, He wept over it, saying: "If thou also hadst known, and that in this thy day, the things that are to thy peace; but now they are hidden from thy eyes." And again: "Jerusalem, Jerusalem, that killest the prophets, and stonest them that are sent unto thee, how often would I have gathered thy children as the bird doth her brood under her wings, and thou wouldst not? Behold your house shall be left unto you desolate."

A lesson surely, and a warning to us all, in every place where He puts His Name, to the end of time; lest we be cold towards His gifts, or unbelieving towards His word, or jealous of His workings, or heartless towards His mercies. Amen.

It would be well if we opened our minds to what is meant by the doctrine of the Son of God dying on the Cross for us.

TRIAL comes after peace. Still God mer-
cifully does grant a respite now and then;
and perhaps He grants it to us the more,
the more careful we are not to abuse it.
For all seasons we must thank Him, for
time of sorrow and time of joy, time of
warfare and time of peace. And the more
we thank Him for the one, the more we
shall be drawn to thank Him for the other.
Each has its own proper fruit, and its own
peculiar blessedness. Yet our mortal flesh
shrinks from the one, and of itself prefers
the other;—it prefers rest to toil, peace to
war, joy to sorrow, health to pain and sick-
ness. When then Christ gives us what is
pleasant, let us take it as a refreshment by
the way, that we may, when God calls, go
in the strength of that meat forty days and
forty nights unto Horeb, the mount of
God. Let us rejoice in Epiphany with
trembling, that at Septuagesima we may
go into the vineyard with the labourers
with cheerfulness, and may sorrow in Lent
with thankfulness; let us rejoice now, not
as if we have attained, but in hope of attaining. Let us take our present happiness,

not as our true rest, but, as what the land of Canaan was to the Israelites,—a type and shadow of it. If we now enjoy God's seasons, let us not cease to pray that they may prepare us for His presence hereafter. If we enjoy the presence of friends, let them remind us of the communion of saints before His throne. Let us trust nothing here, yet draw hope from everything —that at length the Lord may be our everlasting light, and the days of our mourning may be ended. "Our Father who art in Heaven, hallowed be Thy Name, Thy Kingdom come."

TRIUMPHS

BECAUSE IT IS written, "Freely ye have received, freely give," we dare not hide in a napkin those mercies, and that grace of God, which have been given us, not for our own sake only, but for the benefit of others.

Such a zeal, poor and feeble though it be in us, has been the very life of the Church, and the breath of her preachers and missionaries in all ages. It was a fire such as this which brought Our Lord from heaven, and which He desired, which He travailed to communicate to all around Him. "I am come to send fire on the earth," He says, "and what will I, but that it be kindled?"

Such, too, was the feeling of the great Apostle to whom his Lord appeared in order to impart to him this fire. "I send thee to the Gentiles," He had said to him on his conversion, "to open their eyes, that they may be converted from darkness to light, and from the power of Satan unto God." And, accordingly, he at once began to preach to them, "for," as he says, "the charity of Christ constrained him," and he was "made all things to all that he might save all," and he "bore all for the elect's sake, that they might obtain the salvation which is in Christ Jesus, with heavenly glory."

This is why Catholic missionaries throw themselves so generously among the fiercest savages, and risk the most cruel torments, as knowing the worth of the soul, as realizing the world to come, as loving their brethren dearly, though they never saw them, as shuddering at the thought of the eternal woe, and as desiring to increase the fruit of their Lord's passion, and the triumphs of His grace. Thy kingdom come!

LILY

CERTAIN OF THY SAINTS came so close to Thee that they were granted to receive Thee into their breasts; to be the most perfect images that earth has seen of Thy peace and immutability. Such were the many virgin Saints whom history records for our veneration: St. Joseph, the great St. Anthony, St. Cecilia who was waited on by Angels, St. Nicolas of Bari, St. Peter Celestine, St. Rose of Viterbo, St. Catherine of Sienna and a host of others.

Above all, the Virgin of Virgins, and Queen of Virgins, the Blessed Mary, who, though replete and overflowing with the grace of love, yet for the very reason that she was the "seat of wisdom" and the "ark of the covenant," is more commonly represented under the emblem of the lily than of the rose.

Queen of all Saints, pray for us now and in the hour of our death. Amen.

OVERCOMES

THY GRACE can undo the past, it can realise the hopeless. No sinner, ever so odious, but may become a Saint; no Saint, ever so exalted, but has been, or might have been, a sinner. Grace overcomes nature, and grace only overcomes it.

Thy grace triumphed in Magdalen, in Matthew, and in Nicodemus; heavenly grace came down upon corrupt human nature; it subdued impurity in the youthful woman, covetousness in the publican, fear of man in the Pharisee.

The rebellion of my reason, the waywardness of my feelings, the disorder of my thoughts, the fever of passion, the treachery of my senses,—these evils may Thy all-powerful grace subdue in me. Amen.

It is certain that man is not sufficient for his own happiness, that he is not himself, is not at home with himself, without the presence within him of the grace of Him who, knowing it, has offered that grace freely.

May He who is Omnipotent and Omniscient, touch many hearts at once and in many places. Amen.

ENDOWMENTS

THY VERY PRESENCE enkindled Peter's heart and at once drew him unto Thee. When he saw Thee walking on the sea, his first impulse was to leave the vessel and hasten to Thy side: "Lord, if it be Thou, bid me come to Thee upon the waters." On another occasion, when many of the disciples fell away, and "Jesus said to the twelve, Do you wish to go away?" St. Peter answered, "Lord, to whom shall we go? Thou art Christ, the Son of God."

Thou didst love Peter not simply because he was Thy Apostle, but because Peter had that intense, unearthly love of Thee and that faith which flesh and blood could not exercise, which were the fitting endowments of an Apostle. May I, in St. Peter's words, be "the hidden man of the heart."

OF THE STORM

IF JESUS loved John, it was not as merely one of the Twelve, but because he was adorned with the special gift of supernatural chastity. If He loved Mary, Martha and Lazarus, it was not only as His friends and guests, but for their burning charity and their pure contrition and their self-sacrificing devotion. I am really dead though I seem to live, unless I am grafted upon the True Vine and am partaker of the secret supernatural life which circulates through the undecaying branches. Build Thou the house, lest I labor in vain.

I doubt not that Thou, who couldst tread the billows so securely, can self-sustained bear any weight my weakness throws upon Thee, and can be my immovable refuge and home amid the tossing and tumult of the storm.

As Thou didst say in the Old Testament, "Lift up thy eyes round about; lift up thy eyes and see. All these are gathered together, they are come to Thee . . . Thus saith the Lord God . . . Behold I will lift up my hand to the Gentiles, and will set up my standard to the people."

Thou didst say in the New Testament, "O thou of little faith, why didst thou doubt?" With those that were in the boat, I adore Thee saying: Indeed Thou art the Son of God. Amen.

CORDS OF ADAM

THOU DIDST surround Thyself on Thy coming with so much that was touching and attractive and subduing. Thou didst bid Thy angels proclaim that Thou wast to be seen as a little infant, in a manger and in a Virgin's bosom, at Bethlehem. Thou didst go about doing good. Thou didst die in public, before the world, with Thy mother and Thy beloved disciple by Thee. Thou dost now tell us how exalted Thou art in Heaven with a host of glorified Saints, who are our intercessors, about Thy throne. Thus dost Thou draw us by the "cords of Adam."

Jesu, Thou dost give us Thy own sweet Mother Mary for our mother, the most perfect image after Thyself of what is beautiful and tender and gentle and soothing in human nature. Thou dost manifest Thyself by an ineffable condescension on our Altars, still humbling Thyself, though Thou reignest on high.

Thou dost reclaim us by means of ourselves, so that we should, under the power of Thy grace, become "the instruments of justice unto God." Amen.

SIN could not touch Thy Divine Majesty; but it could assail Thee in that way in which Thou didst allow Thyself to be assailed, that is, through the medium of Thy humanity. The envy of the Pharisees, the treachery of Judas, and the madness of the people, were but the instrument or the expression of the enmity which sin felt towards Eternal Purity as soon as, in infinite mercy towards men, Thou didst put Thyself within its reach.

Jesus, Thou hast exhausted the full chalice, from which at first Thy natural infirmity shrank. The seizure and the arraignment, and the buffeting, and the prison, and the mocking, and the passing to and fro, and the scourging, and the crown of thorns, and the slow march to Calvary, and the crucifixion, these have all come. The satisfaction is completed.

The beauty of Thy sanctity, the sweetness of Thy mercy, the brightness of Thy providences, the thrilling music of Thy voice are the antagonist of the flesh, and the soul's champion against the world and the devil. Thou hast thrown Thy net skilfully, and its subtle threads are entwined round each affection of my heart, and its meshes have been a power of God, "bringing into captivity the whole intellect to the service of Christ."

THY CRUCIFIXION

THOU DIDST BECOME perfect man with body and soul. Thou didst take on Thee a body of flesh and nerves, which admitted of wounds and death, and was capable of suffering. Thou didst take a soul, too, which was susceptible of suffering, and moreover was susceptible of the pain and sorrow which are proper to a human soul.

As Thy atoning passion was undergone in Thy body, so it was undergone in Thy soul also. Thy sufferings in Thy body, Thy seizure, Thy forced journeys to and fro, Thy blows and wounds, Thy scourging, the crown of thorns, the nails, the Cross, they are all summed up in the Crucifix itself; they are represented all at once on Thy sacred flesh, as it hangs before us— and meditation is made easy by the spectacle. Jesus, crucified, have mercy on us. And while Holy Church prays and labors on her own field, may converts, beyond that field, to the surprise of all that know them, those who fear the Church or disown her doctrines, at length give themselves up to her, and proclaim her sovereignty through the overruling Providence of Thy crucifixion. Amen.

GETHSEMANE

WHENCE CAME the first fruits of the passion of the Lamb? In Gethsemane's garden, He rose languidly from the earth. He turned, and lo! there was blood upon His garment and in His footprints. No soldier's scourge had touched His shoulders, nor the hangman's nails His hands and feet. He had bled before His time.

That tormented Heart, the seat of tenderness and love, had begun at length to labor and to beat with vehemence beyond its nature; the red streams rushed forth so copious and fierce as to overflow the veins, and bursting through the pores, they stood in a thick dew over His whole skin; then forming into drops, they rolled down full and heavy, and drenched the ground.

And then when the appointed moment

arrived and Thou didst give the word, as Thy passion had begun with Thy soul, with Thy soul did it end. Thou didst not die of bodily exhaustion, or of bodily pain; at Thy will Thy tormented Heart broke, and Thou didst commend Thy spirit to Thy Father! Grant me St. Paul's love; a love fervent, eager, energetic, active, full of great works, "strong as death," a flame which "many waters could not quench, nor the streams drown," which lasted to the end, when he could say, "I have fought the good fight . . . henceforth is laid up for me the crown of justice, which the Lord will render to me at that day, the just Judge." Amen.

HOUSE OF GOD

IF THE WORLD has its fascinations, so surely has the Altar of the living God. Mary pleads with us, over against them, with her chaste eyes, and offers the Eternal Child for our caress, while sounds of cherubim are heard all around singing from out the fullness of the Divine Glory. Has divine hope no emotion? Has divine charity no transport? "How dear are Thy tabernacles, O Lord of hosts!" "I have chosen to be an abject in the house of my God, rather than to dwell in the tabernacles of sinners." "The Lord, turning, looked on Peter": such is the piercing, soul-subduing look of the Son of man. It is come, it is gone, it has done its work, its abiding work, and the world is at fault to account for it. It sees the result; it has not perceived, it has not eyes to see, Thy Divine Hand!

"King Solomon made himself a litter of the wood of Libanus. The pillars thereof he made of silver, the seat of gold, the going up of purple; the midst he covered with charity for the daughters of Jerusalem. Go forth, ye daughters of Sion, and see King Solomon in the diadem, wherewith his mother crowned him in the days of his espousals and in the day of his heart's joy."

BLOTS OUT

IF I would do works meet for penance, they must proceed from a living flame of charity. If I would secure perseverance to the end, I must gain it by continual loving prayer to the Author and Finisher of faith and obedience.

If I would have a good prospect of His acceptance of me in my last moments, still it is love alone which secures Thy love, and blots out sin. Nothing but charity can enable me to live well or to die well.

May I not stand before Thy judgment-seat in the lot of him who has received great gifts from God, and used them for self; who has shut his eyes, who has trifled with truth, who has been led on by God's grace but stopped short of its scope, who has neared the land of promise, yet not gone forward to take possession of it!

Faith alone reaches to the end, faith only endures. May faith and prayer endure for me in that last dark hour, when Satan urges all his powers and resources against my sinking soul. Amen.

TITLE

THOU DIDST COME on earth, not to take Thy pleasure, not to follow Thy taste, not for the mere exercise of human affection, but simply to glorify Thy Father and to do His will.

Thou didst come charged with a mission, deputed for a work; Thou didst look not to the right nor to the left, Thou didst think not of Thyself, Thou didst offer Thyself up to God. My Lord and my God!

Give me that real delight in Thee, in Thy attributes, in Thy will, in Thy commandments, in Thy service, which Saints possess in such fulness, and which alone can give my soul a comfortable title to the merits of Thy death and passion; that feeling with which the loving soul, on its separation from the body, approaches the judgment-seat of its Redeemer!

"The Spirit and the Bride say, Come; and he that heareth, let him say, Come. And he that thirsteth, let him come: and he that will, let him take of the water of life, freely." Amen.

EVERLASTING MUSIC

I COME TO THEE who art my Life and my All; I come to Thee on the thought of Whom I have lived all my life long. To Thee I gave myself when first I had to take a part in the world; I sought Thee for my chief good early, for early didst

Thou teach me, that good elsewhere there was none. Whom have I in heaven but Thee? whom have I desired on earth, whom have I had on earth but Thee?

Yea, when I shall descend into "a land desert, pathless and without water," I will fear no ill, for Thou art with me. I have seen Thee this day face to face, and it sufficeth; I have seen Thee, and that glance of Thine is sufficient for a century of sorrow, in the nether prison. I will live on that look of Thine, though I see Thee not, till I see Thee again, never to part from Thee. That eye of Thine shall be sunshine and comfort to my weary, longing soul; that voice of Thine shall be everlasting music in my ears. Nothing can harm me, nothing shall discompose me: I will bear the appointed years, till the end comes, bravely and sweetly. Amen.

MAN'S BURDEN

THERE IS no limit to be put to the bounty and power of Thy grace; and that I feel sorrow for my sins, and supplicate Thy mercy, is a sort of pledge to me in my heart, that Thou wilt grant me the good gifts I am seeking. Thou canst do what Thou wilt with the soul of man.

Salutary thought for me who am tempted to pride myself in what I do, and what I am; wonderful news for me who sorrowfully recognise in my heart the vast difference that exists between me and the Saints; and joyful news, because I hate sin, and wish to escape from its miserable yoke, yet am tempted at times to think it impossible.

Thy priests of the New Law condole with us, "because they too are compassed with infirmity." Had Angels been our Priests, they could not have condoled with us, sympathised with us, have had compassion on us, felt tenderly for us, and made allowance for us, as men can.

As Thou Thyself, though Thou couldst not sin, yet even Thou, by becoming man, didst take on Thee, as far as was possible to God, man's burden of infirmity and trial in Thy own person.

Thou, who created and upholdest the universe; who will judge every one of us, have mercy on us. Amen.

MAY I "join with faith, virtue, and with virtue, knowledge, and with knowledge, abstinence, and with abstinence, patience, and with patience, pity, and with pity, love of brotherhood, and with love of brotherhood, charity." Amen.

May I experience the operations of Thy grace, the efficacy of Thy sacraments, the power of prayer, the virtue of holy relics, the Communion of Saints, the glorious intercession of the Mother of God, the care and tenderness of my Guardian Angel. Amen.

Let me know something of the presence of God, the merits of Christ, the intercession of the Blessed Virgin; the virtue of recurring prayers, of frequent confession, of daily Masses; the transforming power of the Most Holy Sacrament, the Bread of Angels.

Let me stay within the walls of the strong city, about which the enemy prowls in vain and outside of which the faithful soul will be too wise to venture. Amen.

AND KEEP IT

THY GLORIES, Blessed Mother, are for the sake of Jesus; we praise and bless thee as the first of creatures, that we may duly confess Him as our sole Creator. Thou hast been made more glorious in thy person than in thy office; thy purity is a higher gift than thy relationship to God. Thy Son pointed out to His disciples thy higher blessedness: "Yea, rather, blessed are they who hear the word of God and keep it."

But idle is our labor, worthless is our toil, ashes is our fruit, corruption is our reward, unless we pursue any undertaking in faith and prayer, and sanctify it by purity of life. "Unless the Lord build the House, they labor in vain who build it."

If thou art called the Mother of God, it is to remind Him that, though He is out of sight, He, nevertheless, is our possession, for He is of the race of man.

If we are devout to Saint Joseph, it is as to His foster-father; and if he is the saint of a happy death, it is because he dies in the hands of Jesus and Mary. Amen.

THOUGHT OF THEE

SAINTLINESS and all its attendants—saintly purity, saintly poverty, heroic fortitude and patience, self-sacrifice for the sake of others, renouncement of the world, the favor of Heaven, the protection of Angels, the smile of the Blessed Virgin, gifts of grace, the interpositions of miracles, the intercommunion of merits—these are the high and precious things, the things to be looked up to, the things to be reverently prayed for.

Let me not only have faith in Thee, but wait on Thee; not only have hope in Thee, but watch for Thee; not only love Thee, but long for Thee; not only obey Thee, but look out, look up earnestly for my reward, which is Thyself. "The time is short."

May I be tender and sensitive in my devotion to Thee; feed on the thought of Thee, hang on Thy words; live in Thy smile, and thrive and grow under Thy hand. Amen.

FAVORED DISCIPLES

WHAT WAS the surprise, what the transport, which came upon the favored disciples, whom on one occasion our Lord took up with Him to the mountain's top. He left the sick world, the tormented, restless multitude, at its foot, and He took them up, and was transfigured before them. "His face did shine as the sun, and His raiment was white as the light." How truly was this a glimpse of Heaven! "Lord, it is good to be here."

Saints of the Transfiguration, St. Peter, St. John, St. James, pray for us that we may repeat your prayer of thanksgiving, "Lord, it is good to be here."

It is a great gain, a great mercy, that those who are sent to preach to us, to receive our confessions, and to advise us, can sympathise with our sin, even though they have not known such sin. They will be tender to us, they will "instruct you in the spirit of meekness," as the Apostle says, "considering themselves lest they also be tempted."

St. Paul, obtain for us through thy prayers that same tenderness and meekness, so that considering ourselves we may not be tempted to pride and vanity. Amen.

STRONGHOLDS

APPEAL to all man's powers and faculties, to his reason, to his prudence, to his moral sense, to his conscience; rouse his fears as well as his love; instruct him in the depravity of sin as well as in Thy mercy; but—the animating principle of his new life, by which it is both kindled and sustained, is the flame of Thy charity. Thy Sacred Heart only is strong enough to burn up the strongholds of pride. Amen.

Take me as I am and use me against myself. Turn my affections into another channel and extinguish all carnal love by infusing Thy heavenly charity. Enter into my heart and persuade it and prevail with it, while Thou dost change it. Amen.

Jesus, meek and humble of heart, make my heart like unto Thine. Amen.

Most Sacred Heart of Jesus, we implore that we may ever love Thee more and more.

Most Sacred Heart of Jesus, have mercy on us. Amen.

MY STANDARD

KINGS have descended from their thrones, the learned have given up their pride of intellect, to become poor monks, to live on coarse fare, to be clad in humble weeds, to rise and pray while others slept, to mortify the tongue with silence, and the limbs with toil and to avow an unconditional obedience to another. May they be my standard of right and good. Amen.

HEAVY AND LADEN

AND O, my brethren, when you have taken the great step, and stand in your blessed lot, as sinners reconciled to the Father you have offended, O then forget not those who have been the ministers of your reconciliation; and as they now pray for you to make your peace with God, so do you, when reconciled, pray for them, that they may gain the great gift of perseverance, that they may continue to stand in the grace in which they trust they stand now, even till the hour of death, lest, perchance, after they have preached to others, they themselves become reprobate.

Pray for them that labor and are heavy laden that they may find rest to their souls; pray for them who now stand to you in Christ's stead, and who speak in Christ's name; for they too, like you, have been saved by Christ's all-saving blood. They too, like you, should be lost sinners, unless Christ had had mercy on them, unless His grace had cleansed them, unless His Church had ministered unto them, unless His Saints had interceded for them.

And may their dwelling be the Holy Mount Of Sion:—in the name of Christ our Lord.

PATRON SAINT

SON OF ADAM, son of my nature, the same by nature, differing only in grace, man, like myself, exposed to temptation, the same temptations, to the same warfare within, and without; with the same three deadly enemies,—the world, the flesh and the devil; with the same human, the same wayward heart: differing only as the power of God had changed and ruled it.

You were not an Angel from Heaven but a man, whom grace, and grace alone,

had made to differ from me. You preached
not yourself, but Jesus Christ our Lord.

My patron, Saint ——, pray for me.

TWO JOHNS

O HOW IMPOSSIBLE it is worthily to
conceive of the sanctity of these two
Johns, the Evangelist and the Baptist,
great servants of God, so different is their
whole history in their lives and in their
deaths, yet agreeing together in their se-
clusion from the world, in their tranquillity, and in their all but sinlessness! Mortal sin had never touched them, and we
may well believe that even from deliberate venial sin they were ever exempt.

May we, like them, live in a world of
our own, uniform, serene, abiding; in
visions of peace, in communion with
heaven, in anticipation of glory, speaking
to the world without as from a sacred
shrine, as "a voice crying in the wilderness" or "in the spirit on the Lord's
Day."

St. John the Baptist, pray for us. St.
John the Evangelist, pray for us. Amen.

PURITY prepares the soul for love, and love confirms the soul in purity. The flame of love will not be bright unless the substance which feeds it be pure and unadulterated; and the most dazzling purity is but iciness and desolation unless it draws its life from fervent love.

Love and purity can never be separated. St. Peter, Saint of love, St. John, Saint of purity, pray for us.

I will be content with nothing short of the fruition of my Creator; I will watch for nothing else than the face of my Deliverer.

With St. Peter, of one thing I am not ignorant that one day with the Lord is as a thousand years, and a thousand years as one day . . . looking for and awaiting unto the coming of the day of the Lord.

With St. Paul, I pray that there is laid up for me a crown of justice; and not only to me but to those also who love His coming. Amen.

St. Peter, pray for us. St. Paul, pray for us. Amen.

ABOVE

ALL OF US live in a world which promises well, but does not fulfil; and all of us
begin with hope, and end with disappointment. Doubtless, there is much difference in our respective trials here,
arising from difference of tempers and
fortunes. Still it is in our nature to begin
life thoughtlessly and joyously; to seek
great things in one way or other; to have
vague notions of good to come; to love
the world, and to believe its promises,
and seek satisfaction and happiness from
it. And, as it is our nature to hope, so it is
our lot, as life proceeds, to encounter disappointment.

Thou dost still live, Thou hast ever
lived, who was once upon earth, who
died, who disappeared, who said Thou
wouldst come again. When Thou went
up on high from Mount Olivet, Thy
Apostles kept looking up into heaven;
and it needed Angels to send them to
their work, before they gave over. And
ever after, still it was *Sursum corda* with
them. May I ever seek the things that are
above, where Thou art sitting.

TO ANSWER FOR

MAN IS NOT sufficient for his own happiness; he is not happy except the Presence of God be with him. When he was created, God breathed into him that supernatural life of the Spirit which is his true happiness: and when he fell, he lost the divine gift, and with it his happiness also.

Ever since he has been unhappy; ever since he has a void within him which needs filling, and he knows not how to fill it. He scarcely realizes his own need: only his actions show that he feels it, for he is ever restless when he is not dull and insensible, seeking in one thing or another that blessing which he has lost.

He is truly and really born of God in whom the Divine seed takes root. Neglect not the gift that is in you: neglect not the blessing which by God's free grace you have, and others have not. There is nothing to boast in, that you are God's people; rather the thought is an anxious one; you have much more to answer for.

Lead us not into temptation, but deliver us from evil. Amen.

PERSEVERE in the narrow way. The Prophets and Apostles went through sufferings to which ours are mere trifles; violence and craft combined to turn them aside, but they kept right on, and are at rest.

When the Eternal Son of God came among us, He might have taken our nature, as Adam received it, from the earth, and have begun His human life at mature age; He might have been molded under the immediate hand of the Creator; He need have known nothing of the feebleness of infancy or the slow growth of manhood. This might have been had He so willed; but no; He preferred the penance of taking His place in the line of Adam, and of being born of a woman.

The whole Church of God, from the days of Christ to the present, has been ever held in shame and contempt by men of this world.

It is the Presence of Christ which makes us members of Christ: "neither shall they say, Lo here! and Lo there! for the kingdom of God is within us."

Our Father, who art in heaven, hallowed be Thy name, Thy kingdom come, Thy will be done on earth as it is in heaven.

DAY OF JOY

WHEN MAN was created, then His Maker breathed into him the supernatural life of the Holy Spirit, which is his true happiness; when he fell, he forfeited the divine gift, and with it his happiness also.

But Christ's birth changed all this. Take this thought with you, my brethren, to your homes on this festive day; let them be with you in your family and social meetings. It is a day of joy: it is good to be joyful—it is wrong to be otherwise. For one day we may put off the burden of our polluted consciences, and rejoice in the perfections of our Saviour Christ, without thinking of ourselves, without thinking of our own miserable uncleanness; but contemplating His glory, His holiness, His purity, His majesty, His overflowing love. We may rejoice in the Lord, and in all His creatures see Him. We may enjoy His temporal bounty, and partake the pleasant

things of earth with Him in our thoughts;
we may rejoice in our friends for His sake,
loving them most especially because He
has loved them.

With St. Paul we recall that God has
not appointed us unto wrath, but to obtain
salvation through our Lord Jesus Christ,
who died for us, that whether we wake
or sleep, we should live together with
Him. Amen.

PURGATORY

DEAR ANGEL, say,
Why have I now no fear at meeting Him?
Along my earthly life, the thought of death
And judgment was to me most terrible.
Now that the hour is come, my fear is fled;
And at this balance of my destiny,
Now close upon me, I can forward look
With a serenest joy.

UNTIL THE DAY

NOW let the golden prison ope its gates,
Making sweet music, as each fold revolves
Upon its ready hinge. And ye, great powers,
Angels of Purgatory, receive from me
My charge, a precious soul, until the day,
When from all bond and forfeiture released,
I shall reclaim it for the courts of light.

GUARDIAN ANGEL

MY work is done,
   My task is o'er,
      And so I come,
      Taking it home,
For the crown is won,
     Alleluia,
For evermore.

My Father gave
   In charge to me
      This child of earth
      E'en from its birth,
To serve and save,
     Alleluia,
And saved is he.

This child of clay
   To me was given,
      To rear and train
      By sorrow and pain
In the narrow way,
     Alleluia,
From earth to heaven.

YET QUICKENED

AND these two pains, so counter and so keen,
The longing for Him, when thou seest Him not;
The shame of self at thought of seeing Him,
Will be thy veriest, sharpest purgatory.

*   *   *   *

O happy suffering soul! for it is safe,
Consumed, yet quicken'd, by the glance of God.

[330]

SWIFTLY

SOFTLY and gently, dearly-ransom'd soul,
In my most loving arms I now enfold thee,
And, o'er the penal waters, as they roll,
I poise thee, and I lower thee, and hold thee.

And carefully I dip thee in the lake,
And thou, without a sob or a resistance,
Dost through the flood thy rapid passage take,
Sinking deep, deeper, into the dim distance.

Angels to whom the willing task is given,
Shall tend, and nurse, and lull thee, as thou liest;
And Masses on the earth, and prayers in heaven,
Shall aid thee at the Throne of the Most Highest.

Farewell, but not for ever! brother dear,
Be brave and patient on thy bed of sorrow;
Swiftly shall pass thy night of trial here,
And I will come and wake thee on the morrow.

*   *   *   *

Look, O Lord, upon Thy servants and on
Thy work: and direct their children. And
let the beauty of the Lord our God be
upon us: and the work of our hands, estab-
lish Thou it.

IRKSOMENESS

THE QUARREL of the ancient heathen
with Christianity was that instead of simply fixing the mind on the fair and the
pleasant, it intermingled other ideas with
them of a sad and painful nature; that it

[331]

spoke of tears before joy, a cross before a crown; that it laid the foundation of heroism in penance; that it made the soul tremble with the news of Purgatory and Hell; that it insisted on views and a worship of the Deity, which to their minds was nothing else than mean, servile and cowardly.

The notion of an All-perfect, Everpresent God, in whose sight we are less than atoms, and who, while He deigns to visit us, can punish as well as bless, was abhorrent to them; they made their own minds their sanctuary, their own ideas their oracle, and conscience in morals was parallel to genius in art, and wisdom in philosophy.

But, Thou, O Lord, didst set up Thy personal banner of humility by Thy long imprisonment, before Thy birth, in the womb of the Immaculate Mary.

There was He in His human nature, Who, as God, is everywhere; there was He, as regards His human soul, conscious from the first with a full intelligence, and feeling the extreme irksomeness of the prisonhouse, full of grace as it was.

Jesus, meek and humble of heart, make our hearts like unto Thine!

[332]

THY SIGHT

WHEN a body of missionaries come into a neighborhood to them unknown, strangers to strangers, and there set themselves down, and raise an altar, and open a school, and invite, or even exhort all men to attend them, it is natural that they who see them, and are drawn to think about them, should ask the questions: What brings them hither? Who bids them come? What do they want? What do they preach? What is their warrant? What do they promise?

Many there are who would promptly and confidently answer it, according to their own habitual view of things, on their own principles, the principles of the world. The views, the principles, the aims of the world are very definite, are everywhere acknowledged, and are incessantly acted on. They supply an explanation of the conduct of individuals, whoever they be, ready at hand.

So it has been from the beginning; the Jews preferred to ascribe the conduct of our Lord and His forerunner to any motive but that of a desire to fulfil the will of

God. To the Jews they were, as He says, "like children sitting in the market-place." And then He goes on to account for it: "I thank Thee, Father, Lord of heaven and earth, that Thou hast hid these things from the wise and prudent, and hast revealed them to little ones. Yea, Father; for so hath it been pleasing to Thy sight."

THAT BLOOD

THY CHURCH teaches that man was originally made in God's image, was God's adopted son, was the heir of eternal glory, and, in foretaste of eternity, was partaker here on earth of great gifts and manifold graces; and she teaches that now he is a fallen being. He is under the curse of original sin; he is deprived of the grace of God; he is a child of wrath; he cannot attain to heaven, and he is in peril of sinking into hell.

He is not fated to perdition by some necessary law; he cannot perish without his own real will and deed; and God gives him, even in his natural state, a multitude of inspirations and helps. But it is no light, nor ordinary succor, by which man is

[334]

taken out of his own hands and defended against himself. He requires an extraordinary remedy. Now what a thought is this! what a light does it cast upon man's present state! how different from the view which the world takes of it; how piercing, how overpowering in its influence on the hearts that admit it. The world rejects the Presence of the Word Incarnate, which diffuses sweetness, and tranquillity, and chastity over the heart—is it a thing to be marveled at, that we pray for the world, for which Christ died, and try to convert it to Him and to His Church? We are sure that the Most Holy Redeemer has shed His blood for all men, is it not a very plain and simple consequence that we, His servants, His brethren, His priests, should be unwilling to see that blood shed in vain —wasted I may say, as regards others, and should wish to make them partakers of those benefits which have been vouchsafed to ourselves?

REMEMBER SUCH A ONE

AND, O my brethren, O kind and affectionate hearts, O loving friends, should you know any one whose lot it has been, by writing or by word of mouth, in some degree to help you thus to act; if he has ever told you what you knew about yourselves, or what you did not know; has read to you your wants or feelings, and comforted you by the very reading; has made you feel that there was a higher life than this daily one, and a brighter world than that you see; or encouraged you, or sobered you, or opened a way to the inquiring, or soothed the perplexed; or what he has said or done has ever made you take interest in him, and feel well inclined towards him; remember such a one in time to come, though you hear him not, and pray for him, that in all things he may know God's will, and at all times he may be ready to fulfill it. Amen.

INDEX OF FIRST LINES

INDEX TO TITLES